Funny Business Solutions

&

The Art of Using Humor Constructively

by

Bob Ross

457 actual stories of supremely unique results achieved by
well-known people and companies by thinking funny

Arrowhead Publishing
San Diego, California

Funny Business Solutions: The Art of Using Humor Constructively

Published by Arrowhead Publishing

ISBN 0-9623819-1-8

Printed in the United States of America.

DEDICATION

To my three daughters, Rhonda, Desiree and Kelly, who exemplify the value of humor in everyday situations, and to all those who have contributed to this book by providing material and in sharing my passion for living, loving and laughing.

ACKNOWLEDGMENTS

The material used to write this book was compiled from various news sources, much of which was sent to me over the years by friends and colleagues who know my penchant for gathering stories that illustrate the utilitarianism of humor.

Some of the items used were gleaned from radio and television while others were given to me with no original source indicated. Other anecdotes were related orally by fellow professional speakers and friends.

I wish to thank all those who have provided this material. I regret that I am unable to recognize the specific source for some of the contributions used to compile this book.

While all the related anecdotes are believed to be true, the author cannot guarantee their validity. Without Bob MacKenzie, Dan Conway and my many other friends, colleagues and family members who continually take the time to clip and mail items related to various humor solutions, I would not have been able to write this book.

I wish to give a special thanks to my tennis partner and editor, Jack Moore, who massaged this material into a flowing narrative that had even me reading and enjoying my *own stuff*. His creative editing was augmented by the illustrations in the book.

TABLE OF CONTENTS

Preface

Back in the early 1970s I was the executive director of a large community redevelopment corporation in Lansing, Michigan. There was an occasion when I needed to discuss a matter with the City Planning Director. I tried contacting him by phone but could never catch him in his office. I left messages but my calls were never returned. Finally, I became angry. I began composing in my mind a blistering letter chastising him for his rudeness.

But, happily, before my fingers touched the keyboard of my typewriter I came to a realization. Such a letter would surely make him defensive and hostile and undermine the very reason I was trying to contact him. So I reverted to the humor solution. I sent him a telegram. Who ever heard of anyone ignoring a telegram? In the urgent staccato rhythm of the medium I informed him that I had "found it easier to get an audience with the Pope. Stop. Than to speak with him. Stop."

The next day I got his phone call. He was still laughing at my missive. We joked back and forth and had a very amicable discussion. Once again, the humor

1

solution had worked for me! Humor comes from the Latin word "umere," which means "to be fluid, like in water." As such, humor allows us to reframe situations in a positive light and in a different perspective. I have used this principle many times in my own life.

Telemarketing is an absolute necessity in my profession as a speaker/entertainer but there was a time when I hated it. I decided to try the humor solution and as soon as I began to make it fun, I became better at it; and more successful. It's really not difficult to see why. I was more relaxed on the phone. I related better to the person on the other end of the line. There was more passion in my voice and more enthusiasm in my message. Because I was relaxed and more comfortable talking with prospects, humorous thoughts came easier to me. Occasionally, I would call a business and ask for a person who had been gone for several years. When informed of their departure, I'd say, "Gee, I've got to get up-to-date on things! Is Jimmy Carter still doing a good job in the White House?"

Sharing humor with the person on the other end tended to open them up. A certain rapport was established and they became more receptive to my ideas. I've used this with my tennis game. When I become bogged down and angry with myself for unwarranted mistakes, I retreat to the thought that I'm healthy, happy and there for fun. I remember that exercise is my primary purpose for being on the court. The fun philosophy carries me through the match — always resulting in better performance.

Humor arouses the nervous system

Before I get up to speak to an audience, I think of something funny. It makes me smile, which improves my appearance. It relaxes me and creates positive feelings, resulting in self-energizing behavior.

Humor always generates a positive emotion. And positive emotions can be used to influence the outcomes of many situations. At first glance this might appear to be somewhat mysterious. How can attitude create physical results? But looked at more closely, it makes perfect sense. Speaker Fred Pryor refers to our two extreme mental states as "self-obstructing behavior" (SOB) and "self-energizing behavior" (SEB). He explains that these create an aura within which we function. SOB begets feelings of fear, despair and hopelessness. SEB, on the other hand, stimulates positive sensations of hope, confidence and energy. These influence our behavior and energized behavior creates results while obstructive behavior impedes our performance.

Research has shown that an image in the mind arouses the nervous system. If that is not enough reason to use humor and to try to maintain SEB, consider the words of Will Rogers, the great American humorist. "We're only here for a relatively very short time," Rogers said. "We've got to learn to have a little fun and not take ourselves so seriously."

Getting the message across

What would you guess is the most often repeated and most ignored message in America? I suggest it is the airline safety lecture that we all hear every time we fly commercially. Virtually nobody pays attention to this litany of advice and admonitions, always begun with detailed instructions as to the basic mechanics of a seat belt. Not long ago I was on a flight aboard a Southwest Airlines' plane. This is a company known for injecting fun into every aspect of its operation. As the plane lifted off, a male voice came over the intercom. It was an imitation of Mr. Rogers, of the children's beloved *Mr. Rogers' Neighborhood.*

"Hello boys and girls," he mimicked, "welcome to the neighborhood." He went on to deliver the safety message in that voice and manner.

"In case of a loss of cabin pressure, you'll either be sucked out of the window, or you'll be sitting there staring at four dangling oxygen masks. If you don't have yours on, boys and girls, you're not doing it right. And in the unlikely event of a water landing, your seat cushion turns into a flotation device. Boys and girls, can you say, 'shark attack?'"

When he finished this highly humorous directive, virtually all the passengers applauded. This is testimony to the power of humor in communications. By utilizing comedy, he focused attention, heightened interest and made his message palatable through entertainment. He made it more memorable and established rapport with his audience. Because they were laughing with him, they were more open to his message. He had a high likability factor — even though he was not visible to most of the passengers.

Do you have a message you would like to get across better? Try reaching for the humor solution. Humor can take us places and do things for us that are uniquely advantageous. When, after a couple of months, I couldn't get one of my clients to send their check for my expenses (in connection with a speaking engagement) I became irritated. But instead of sending the usual dunning notice expressing my disappointment with their dilatory behavior, I decided to draw on my sense of humor. In keeping with the nature of my business I sent the following note:

> *Barbara,*
> *This is in regard to an amount owing of $174.53. Two*
> *months have passed since the services were furnished and*

the amount became due. Besides impairing your credit rating, our ties to organized crime could mean serious injury to you. Broken limbs can be a serious impediment to enjoying the holiday season. Please don't make us send Bruno over to Des Moines. In this weather, such trips away from the sunny environs of southern California make him very unhappy and this is usually reflected by big time bruises and ugly compound fractures. Please let us hear from you!

    Happy Holidays,
    Bob Ross

The money was received shortly thereafter and Barbara called to laugh about the letter. Goodwill was retained and the purpose was achieved. Humor is the only tool I can think of that would have accomplished both objectives. Another time I was unsuccessful in collecting some money due me for a speaking engagement, I sent the following letter:

As you can see from the enclosures, Lyn, I'm a bona fide member of the Procrastinators Club of America. As such, I am sworn to recommend for membership only those people who are first-class procrastinators. You will note that I have enclosed a membership application. However, before you get around to filling it out (if you ever do), I'd be grateful if you would take the time to mail my check for the comedy roast I did for your group. In the delightful event that you have already sent the check, along with your letter telling the world how wonderful I am, then I am most grateful and my recommendation for membership stands. After all, if you had heard my talk on Murphology, you would know that bills travel through the mail at two and a half times the speed of checks.

    Best regards,
    Bob Ross

This technique can be easily replicated. I read about a florist who, after several billings, had been unable to collect on some credit extended to a customer. One day the florist called the delinquent patron, introduced himself and began singing "Happy Birthday." Surprised, the man assured him it wasn't his birthday.

"I know," he replied, "but your bill is one year old today!"

Experience has taught me that, in dealing with people, there are usually several ways to achieve your purpose. The most overlooked is the one that is usually the most effective and appropriate — the humor solution. In addition to being the elixir of life, humor is often the ideal solution to life's many perplexing situations. This book contains many stories illustrating the use of humor as a successful solution to various problems.

The book suggests methods you can use to put the magical power of humor to work as a strategy for success in your personal and professional life. But it is not just about humor. It includes the use of fun and play as well as the family of associated theatrics, which can be used to accomplish anything and overcome any hurdle.

Humor can make your life healthier, happier and more productive. You'll find many anecdotes in every chapter, but they are not there just to make the point or just to explain by example. They are included because I believe that if you learn to think laterally — to imbed the validity of humor in your mind — and then use that as a reference point, you will begin to develop your own methods to accomplish the very same thing.

My hope is that this book will broaden your awareness of the many uses of humor; that it will help you to be more effective and enrich your life by adding the humor solution to your arsenal of skills.

"Humor is the only divine quality of Man"

—C.G. Jung

Chapter One

Enhance Your Likability Factor

"If you wish to glimpse inside a human soul and get to know a man,
don't bother analyzing his ways of being silent, of talking, of weeping,
or seeing how much he is moved by noble ideas;
you'll get better results if you just watch him laugh.
If he laughs well, he's a good man."
—Fyodor Dostoyevsky

The late Brandon Tartikoff was known as Hollywood's crown prince. He was a shameless showman who would do anything for a laugh. Although it was his personality that made him uniquely beloved in a tough town, he was one of the smartest, funniest and, as it turned out, youngest top people in Hollywood; having taken over NBC at age thirty-one. In an industry where most people are happy for any kind of job, he had more than one studio begging him to join them.

Tartikoff had wit. And he knew how to use it to make things happen. In 1988, legendary television producer Aaron Spelling was thinking of leaving

ABC after twelve years. As *Newsweek* relates it, CBS owner Laurence Tisch flew in from New York to woo him at one of Hollywood's oldest, most formal and finest restaurants. The two men had barely sat down when the waiter began some really wacky behavior. He stuck his finger in the wine bottle, licked it and said, "Mmm — pretty good." Then he began to make more unusual remarks. "Hey, you guys gonna order? I got a hot date." Next he started making comments about CBS's prime-time schedule. Tisch and Spelling were shocked and uncomfortable. Finally, the waiter removed his mustache, goatee, and glasses. It was Brandon Tartikoff, head of NBC. Spelling was reeled in soon after.

The "likability factor"

More than anything else your image is enhanced by your "likability factor." One day White House spokesman Michael McCurry arrived at his daily press briefing to find on his lectern a paper bag with a face scribbled on it. He put the bag over his head and told the assembled newsies the day's information was coming from "an anonymous source." Such shenanigans send the massage, "I don't take myself too seriously," and go a long way toward boosting his image with the press corps.

Some years ago, my friend Ron Dentinger was voted the funniest person in Wisconsin. He is a columnist for the *Dodgeville Gazette* and a humorous speaker. Most issues of *Reader's Digest* contain his quips and quotes.

"How are you, Ron?" I asked.

Gently patting his ample paunch, he replied, "Well, as you can see, Bob, I'm able to take nourishment quite well!"

By using some good natured humor pointed at himself, Ron's likability factor soars.

William Buckley, popular newspaper columnist and host of television's *Firing Line*, noticed President Nixon taking notes during an informal conversation. Buckley felt extraordinarily flattered "even though I knew there was the possibility that he could have been writing, 'I wish this bore would finish and get out of here!'" This makes two statements about Buckley. First, presidents do indeed seek his counsel, and second, he doesn't take himself too seriously.

Late Show host David Letterman says, "You see a lot of really good-looking women with dorky-looking guys. It hasn't worked in my case." When Tony Randall, 77, was asked to comment on the marriage of Woody Allen, 62, to Soon-Yi Previn, 27, Randall, whose wife is also 27, said, "She's too old for him."

Former presidential cabinet member Robert Reich is a liberal who opened his speeches by joking about his four-foot, ten-inch height. "Do I look like big government," he would ask.

When he was U.S. Attorney General, Robert Kennedy would personally welcome young lawyers to his staff. "This may appear to be a large organization," he would say, "but when you do something well, I'll hear about it and it'll go on your record. I want you to recall that I was recently a lowly worker in the Justice Department myself but that I now serve as Attorney General, due to perseverance, long hours, hard work and the fact that my brother became President of the United States — not necessarily in that order."

In these cases the ice was broken with the audience by calling attention to something that would not otherwise go unnoticed. But, by using it to their advantage, they cleverly won over their audiences, whether it was a large group or an individual. Just letting people know you have a sense of humor goes a long way toward endearing yourself to others.

Perception is reality

"Humor is the hole that lets the sawdust out of a stuffed shirt."
—Anon.

It is said that each of us is three people. We are the person *we think we are*, the person *others think we are*, and the person *we really are*.

Success, as measured by the public's acceptance, has to do primarily with what *others think we are*. Our image, or the image of our business, is reality. People act on what they perceive. We can enhance that perception by using humor.

The more important the person, the more meaningful the self-deprecating humor. When Margaret Thatcher was Prime Minister of England she was once walloped on the head with a bunch of flowers by an angry woman. Responded Thatcher, "It was so hard on the daffodils." Famous newsman Edward R. Murrow dismissed his celebrity status by commenting, "Just because your voice reaches halfway around the world doesn't mean you are wiser than when it reached only to the end of the bar."

It never hurts to poke a little fun at yourself and it lets people know you don't take yourself too seriously. This can include diminishing the importance of your success. Billionaire Jean Paul Getty was once asked the secret of his success. Said Getty, "Some people find oil. Others don't."

It also includes slipping in some unexpected humor. Conrad Hilton, hotelier extraordinaire, was asked on national television if he had one vital message for

Americans. Turning to the cameras, he said, "Please — place the curtains *inside* the tub."

Fashion a quip around a trait

You, too, can use the technique of building yourself up by putting yourself down. Select a physical characteristic or a personality trait and fashion a quip around it. The personality trait can be real or imagined. Many show business people have contrived images that are used to facilitate their stage personae. Foster Brooks has an entire act based on his drinking, but he is a teetotaler. Red Skelton always had a cigar in his mouth that was only slightly shorter than a telephone pole, but he never smoked. It was a prop. Jack Benny was, in real life, an extremely generous man. He gave liberally to many charities. But his stage persona was that of a very stingy man and there were numerous jokes about his frugality.

Benny used that false reputation as the theme for numerous radio shows and ultimately to his resounding success as an entertainer. He is said to have gotten the longest recorded laugh. It came during his radio show when he was approached on the street by a mugger. The mugger insists, "Give me your money or your life." There follows a long extended pause, after which Benny says, "I'm thinking, I'm thinking."

Colin Powell, former head of the Joint Chiefs of Staff, likes to tell how frightened he was before the numerous parachute jumps he had to make during airborne training. He sheds the grandiose self-image of a four-star general with self-mocking jokes.

Kemmons Wilson, founder of Holiday Inns, was asked how he could do so well never having been to college. He replied, "When you don't have an education, you have to use your brains."

Developing your own self-directed put-down

If you are in a situation where your attributes are being touted, take a page from the late, great Dizzy Dean, who said, "The Good Lord was good to me. He gave me a strong body, a good right arm and a weak mind." Acknowledging your shortcoming lets folks know you consider yourself to be just as human as they are. Such tactics include relating self-deprecating stories about yourself. Dan Quayle enhanced his image by telling the story about the time he was driving home after picking up his daughter from school. At a red light, a motorist pulled alongside and rolled down his window. "You're a double for Dan Quayle!" he shouted. "Gee, I hope I don't look like that guy," Quayle replied, jokingly. "Yeah," the man shot back. "I know what you mean."

Frank Sinatra was a superstar who displayed his sense of humor in a self-deprecating way. The "Chairman of the Board" had a hard, no-nonsense image but softened it by poking a little fun at himself. Sinatra used to tell a story on himself about the time comedian Don Rickles approached his table at a Las Vegas restaurant to ask a favor. Rickles was dining with a friend and wanted to impress her. Would Sinatra please make a point of stopping by his table to say hello? Sinatra obliged; he walked across the restaurant, slapped Rickles on the back and told him how delighted he was to see him. Rickles, in full character, responded, "Beat it, Frank. This is personal."

Country-western singer Mel Tillis stutters when he talks, but surprisingly, not when he sings. Larry King says he makes a charming interview guest by being candid and joking about the problem. He says Tillis comes across as being completely at ease with himself and puts others at ease by addressing his problem with the humor solution.

Choosing a good flaw

Suppose you're tall. You can quip that you are the first one to know it's raining. Conversely, if you're very short you can joke that you are the last to know when it's raining. Or you can tell people that you worked your way through school standing on wedding cakes.

Someone who is bald can crack jokes about being "follically challenged." A person with a very large nose can use one or more of several self-deprecating lines. He can say that all of his pullover shirts have stretch marks. Or, he can say he went sailing and when he turned around the ship changed course.

The trait you select doesn't even have to be a flaw; anything unusual can be used for a highly ingratiating, self-deprecating remark. If you're noticeably older than your audience you can get some laughter by doing a short routine on it. "My social security number is three. I almost wasn't able to be here tonight: I was scheduled to attend my class reunion, but the other guy couldn't make it! One thing about being my age: there's very little peer pressure, and you're not bothered by life insurance agents. When I play golf, they make me settle up after every hole. My doctor told me not to buy any green bananas."

If you're particularly young for your position or station in life, a similarly self-effacing series of comic remarks will create smiles and put you in good stead with your audience or companions. San Diego school board candidate Daniel Smiechowski plays off his unpronounceable name by announcing that he had shortened it to help with voter identification. He explains by saying he'll now go by "*Dan* Smiechowski."

11

Whatever it is that makes you unique, unless you are particularly handsome, pretty or well-built, poke a little fun at yourself and turn it into an asset. Who can forget presidential candidate Ross Perot during the 1992 debates. He used homilies and humor throughout the campaign to elevate his image and it worked. During one of the debates, someone offered an idea and Perot made the remark, "I'm all ears." Since he has rather large ears, the comment evoked much laughter and did a lot to enhance his image among the voters.

Oliver North, the small and slightly-built marine officer who was the center of attention for his allegedly surreptitious dealings, was asked who should play him in a movie. He said, "I was thinking of Sylvester Stallone, but I don't think he's got the body."

California Governor Pete Wilson suffers from a chronic throat problem that affects his voice. When he spoke to the Rotary Club it was telling. Wilson handled it by saying that, as a fiscal conservative, he shopped around and got a real bargain, but that would be the last time he would have throat surgery done at a place called "Tonsils 'R' Us."

Political office almost demands a sense of humor. As Meg Greenfield put it in an article in *Newsweek* magazine: "A true sense of humor — specifically including a sense of humor about oneself — is not merely a fringe benefit or a nice add-on in a person aspiring to hold high public office. It is a pretty reliable indicator that its proprietor knows what is serious because he or she knows what is funny. It is a precondition of true sympathy and compassion for one's fellow creatures — as distinct from political-platform 'sympathy' and 'compassion,' which so often come from the costume-rental store."

You'll recall that President Reagan was also very good at making fun of himself. He would often make humorous comments about his age, his memory, and his Hollywood background.

Leaving a legacy of laughter

George Bush lost his incumbency largely on his failure to honor the promise, "Read my lips — no new taxes." When he was asked about life after the presidency, he said, "Well, for one thing, I find that I no longer win every golf game I play." His son George, governor of Texas, apparently has his father's sense of humor. When his wife urged him to buy new formal wear for an upcoming press dinner, he reportedly told her, "Read my lips — no new tuxes." A pun, but a pretty good one. (And since it was self-effacing, permissible.)

Adlai Stevenson responded to his electoral defeat by Dwight Eisenhower in the 1950s by saying, "It hurts too much to laugh and I'm too old to cry." What do you do after you suffer a big public loss? If you're smart, you recover some of the lost dignity with self-deprecating humor. If ridicule is the worst enemy of pompous politicians, then humor must be the best friend of successful ones.

A number of very successful politicians have left a legacy of laughter in their political wakes. Mo Udall, the former Secretary of the Interior, spent thirty years in congress and developed a reputation for self-directed humor. His life was anchored by adversity (he lost an eye in a childhood accident and later developed Parkinson's disease) but he maintained unswerving optimism manifested by self-targeted jocularity and good cheer. In 1970, vying with Hale Boggs for the post of House majority leader, Udall and his supporters sported "MO" lapel pins as they confidently entered the Democratic Caucus. But when the tables turned in favor of Boggs, Udall gave a gracious concession speech and expressed his pain by turning his pin upside down so it read, "OW."

Doing your own image make-over

One of the best case studies to illustrate the power of humor in image enhancement is that of former U.S. senator and presidential candidate Bob Dole. During his 1996 campaign for president he was saddled with the problem of having the image of a curmudgeon. Some of this was due to the natural set of his face and a rather dull public persona. It was also due in part to having been known as a hatchet man in 1976 when he was Gerald Ford's running mate. Dole was also considered mean-spirited in 1988 when he told President George Bush to "quit lying about my record." He tried to overcome that reputation by using humor in his debates with President Bill Clinton but it didn't seem to take hold. When he fell off the platform at a California campaign event, he joked that he was trying to do "that new Democratic dance, the Macarena." It was only after the campaign was over that his real sense of humor came through. And it proved to be substantial. It was one of the best and most publicized image make-overs ever. His likability factor soared!

The vanquished Dole transformed his public image from dour Washington insider to friendly uncle with a sarcastic edge by appearing on *Saturday Night Live* and poking some fun at himself. Playing off his quirky penchant for referring to himself in the third person, he said, "I don't run around saying Bob Dole does this and Bob Dole does that. That's not something Bob Dole does. That's not something Bob Dole has ever done, or that Bob Dole will ever do."

Then, the ex-candidate accused his impersonator, Norm MacDonald, of doing a poor imitation of Dan Ackroyd's classic Dole, and said, "Bob Dole knows how much it meant to you to play him on your show and Bob Dole feels your pain."

Dole joked that he had already found work. "I've got a job answering phones down at the Red Cross. My wife pulled some strings," quipped Dole. He was referring to his wife, Elizabeth, who was about to resume her job as head of the relief agency. Dole continued, "Hello, Red Cross. How may Bob Dole direct your call?"

He appeared in a series of television guest shots and commercials. He swept away the tag of loser and, in fact, *Time* magazine put him in the winner category of its Winners & Losers column. Even former Democratic presidential candidate Michael Dukakis gave Dole a tip of his hat. Not that a sense of humor was new for Dole. In November 1984, he was heralded by the *Washington Post* as witty and humorous. Colleagues were quoted as stating that he and Alan Simpson were the two funniest people in the Senate. But it all got buried under the unseemly business of running for president. His handlers mistakenly forced him to suppress his wit on the campaign trail.

Sweeping away the loser tag

Following his loss, Dole played off his campaign gaffe of referring to the "Brooklyn Dodgers" baseball team (which had left Brooklyn decades ago). He sent a form letter to the reporters who covered his campaign. It read in part, "In any event, please let me know if I can ever be of assistance — maybe get you tickets to a Brooklyn Dodgers game." Dole's post campaign antics, which centered almost entirely on self-deprecating humor, boosted his image considerably.

Vice President Al Gore has a reputation for being "wooden." In campaign speeches while running for reelection in 1996 he enhanced his image by poking a little fun at that aspect of himself. He would ask audiences, "Do you want to see my newest version of the Macarena?" Then, staying momentarily still, he would add, "Do you want to see it again?"

Following the election, Gore went on the banquet circuit. As he warmed up for what most thought would be his own bid for president in 2000, he began to sharpen his humor quotient. While it demonstrates how humor lifts the likability factor, Gore's comedy vehicle also serves as a good example of parlaying topical humor into a module that generates not one but several laughs — each built upon the other.

The V.P. used "history's short list of Democratic vice presidents who have been elected to a second term." Listing them (there are five in addition to him), he ticked off humorous quips about each. Some of his repertoire: John Nance Garner described the office as a spare tire on the automobile of government. Thomas Riley Marshall told the story of two brothers, "one of whom went to sea, the other became vice president. Neither was ever heard from again." Then, capping it off, he told his audience about John C. Calhoun who was known as the "cast-iron man" because of his less-than-casual demeanor. He then asked in mock incredulity, "Can you imagine being so stiff as to be called the 'cast-iron man?'" Talk about building yourself up by tearing yourself down!

When former comedian and singer Sonny Bono was elected to congress in 1994, he was unapologetically dubbed an "idiot savant from way beyond the Beltway" by the *Washington Post.* House staffers secretly referred to him as "Sonny Bonehead." Washington can be a mean place and among the unabashedly snobby political elite Bono was seen as the laughing stock of the GOP's famed Class of '94. But, using his ability to disarm his critics by poking fun at himself, he converted skeptic to friend and became the most sought-after presence at Republican party events. A master of comic relief, he cut through the paralyzing Capitol tension and managed to make an utterly humorless institution laugh at itself. Upon his untimely death in a skiing accident, the Washington elite praised him for his wit and the way he used it to turn Beltway snickers into respect.

One of the fastest and most dramatic image conversions took place in 1974. The Ivy League *Harvard Lampoon* had been making fun of John Wayne for an extended period and finally invited him to their campus to receive their "Brass Balls Award." The "Duke" went to Harvard and in one day turned around the student body with his own brand of self-effacing humor. Riding around in a tank, he poked some fun at himself and answered students' questions with the same good-natured humor. When one questioner asked him where he got the fake hair, Wayne responded: "What fake hair? This is *real* hair. It's not *my* hair, but it's *real hair.*" The movie start got a standing ovation from a crowd that began as extremely hostile.

Going to another level

Similarly, when *Parade Magazine* did a piece on noted sports curmudgeon George Steinbrenner, it referred to him as being 71 years old. Mr. Steinbrenner, in his reply to the magazine, displayed his sense of humor and helped promote an image make-over. The New York Yankees' owner responded, "Although I may look it, and at times most recently have felt it, I am not 71 years old, as your 'Personality Parade' stated on February 2. I am only 66. I plead with you to not hurry along my demise any faster than it already is!" Apparently recognizing the mercenary image that had emerged in the past, Steinbrenner then appeared in a humorous KFC television commercial that poked some fun at his reputation for a hard-boiled management style.

Taking a flaw, whether it be physical, character, reputation or whatever, and turning it into an asset is in keeping with the axiom, "When life gives you lemons, make lemonade." It's a powerful statement that can be absolute magic. This takes us to another level of situational humor solutions.

Even religious leaders need this talent. When University of Wisconsin researchers prepared to undertake a study of great apes, they somehow sent a questionnaire to an actual primate — Archbishop George Cram, primate of the Anglican Church of Canada. His secretary, the Rev. Michael Ingham, displayed his own sense of humor by replying to the inquiry. He pointed out the error and added, "While it is true that our primate occasionally enjoys bananas, I have never seen him walk with his knuckles on the ground or scratch himself publicly under the armpits."

Here is an item from the *San Diego Union-Tribune*: "Former San Diegan Merrill "Tony" McPeak, the Air Force chief of staff, maintains a healthy sense of self for a four-star general. And his self-deprecating humor earned him instant rapport Thursday with his Rotary audience. McPeak, a much-decorated fighter pilot, said it was an honor for a 'lowly pilot' to address them. 'You know' he said, 'they say there are two basic requirements for being a fighter pilot — you have to be short and you have to be stupid. Now I'm a little over the average height. But then sometimes they'll waive the height requirement if you're stupid enough.'" This is one you could adapt to your own profession!

Build yourself up by tearing yourself down

Building yourself up by tearing yourself down works for organizations the same way it works for individuals. Want to talk about an image problem? How about the Internal Revenue Service? When it comes to taxes, most people feel they've been soaked and they'd love a chance to get even. Well, the Southern California District IRS Office played off these feelings and set up a dunking booth in downtown San Diego. For ten years now they've sponsored an annual "Dunk the IRS." For 94 cents, taxpayers get three chances to dunk an IRS agent in a tub of cold water. The proceeds go to the local Leukemia Society. People get an opportunity to let off a little steam in a safe and fun way and the IRS gets an image boost by utilizing the fun/humor solution.

When the city of San Diego sought to renovate their football stadium for the city's "Chargers," a couple of gadflies challenged them in court, jeopardizing not only the stadium expansion but creating the possibility that the city's professional football team might leave town. The gadflies not only lost but became possibly the most disliked folks in town. In an attempt to rehabilitate their image, they offered themselves up for a charity event. The fund raiser was called "Dunk Your Demons" and the minimum bid for participation was $1,000. The good-natured fun helped rebuild their images.

Clever signs of the times

Even state and local governments will use humor on occasion to deal with issues. If you visit Portland, Oregon, and go to SW Salmon Street, you'll find a sculpture of a salmon embedded in the corner wall of the building (as though it came flying through the air and got stopped while penetrating the wall). When Idaho decided to remove what was the only traffic light on Interstate 90 between Boston and Seattle (3,081 miles), they placed it in a coffin and drove it in a hearse to a mock burial site. Nevada State Route 375 is known for its sightings

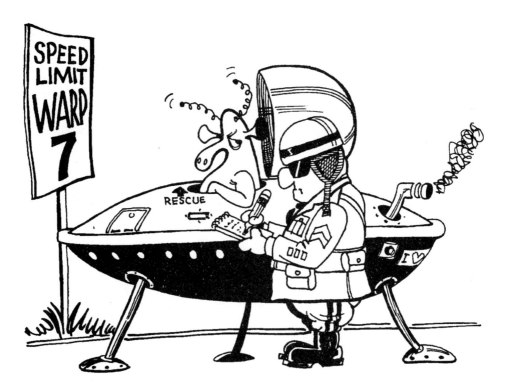

of UFOs. So when they dedicated the road, the state called it the "Extraterrestrial Highway" and Governor Bob Miller personally showed up with the speed restriction sign that called for a limit of "Warp 7." In Canyon City, Texas, there is a sign near the Canyon Lake Dam that reads: "Slow down, See Our Dam; Speed Up, See Our Dam Judge."

A town located a mile off the main highway west of Boston was having a tough time economically. The city fathers held numerous meetings trying to showed up and told them he had the answer. "What is it?" they wanted to know. He said, "We need to put up a billboard out at the junction of the highway." But they responded, "We already have a billboard there!" "In that case," said the salesman, "we'll have to change the copy." He was given permission to do that and soon business began to boom. The message he placed on the large sign read:

> THIS IS THE ROAD
> PAUL REVERE WOULD HAVE TAKEN
> IF HE HAD COME THIS WAY.

If your city or town is remote and undiscovered, a little humor can put it on the map. Take Wisdom, Montana, for instance. The town is virtually unknown. The nearest golf course is miles away. But this little town of only 120 folks will tip its collective cowboy hat to the unlikely but increasingly popular local pastime of golf. They hold the Cow Pasture Open, an intentionally unorthodox tournament played on a makeshift course that, according to *Newsweek*, is a cattle ranch the other 364 days of the year. Wayne Challoner, president of Big Hole Tourism, predicts more than 10,000 visitors from all over the United States will attend the tournament. The course's biggest hazard is cow pies.

This technique of enhancing your image with humor is even more impressive when the subject matter of the put-down is already on the minds of the audience (which in some cases can be only one person). After Pee Wee Herman's arrest for indecent exposure and the avalanche of related jokes that followed, he appeared on television at an awards ceremony. His opening line indirectly acknowledged the situation: "So has anybody heard any good jokes lately?"

Dismissing the issue with humor

President John Kennedy was especially adept at laughing at himself. During his presidential campaign, there was a lot of talk about how his father's enormous wealth was being used to assist him. So when he spoke at a banquet, he used that as the basis for some self-directed humor. He announced that he had received a telegram from his father telling him not to buy a single vote more than necessary to win, adding the admonishment, "I'll be damned if I'm going to pay for a landslide." Known for his heroism as captain of a PT boat during the war, he would dismiss it by assuring people that it was "purely involuntary." This did not detract from his reputation for valor, but actually enhanced his image.

During this same campaign the issue of Kennedy's religion came up. If elected he would become the first Roman Catholic president and some wondered aloud how he might be influenced by the Pope. Kennedy dealt with the issue by using humor to dismiss it. He said, "I asked Cardinal Spellman how to deal with the question of the Pope's infallibility. And Cardinal Spellman said, 'I don't know what to tell you. All I can say is he keeps calling me Spillman.'"

Putting your sense of humor to work can be profitable as well as fun. This is especially true when you've been handed a lemon.

For an example, take the case of a barber shop whose turf was suddenly invaded by two different "discount" competitors selling their services for only four dollars. How do you compete when your market-rate is $10 haircuts? The barber tapped his sense of humor and put out a sign: "WE FIX $4 HAIRCUTS."

Using comic vision

A food distributor was having trouble selling his canned salmon because it was white. Since most salmon is pink, how do you market white salmon? Using comic vision, he designed his label to read: "Our salmon guaranteed not to turn pink in the can."

Humor works in all aspects of life. Illinois State Representative Ellis Levin mailed a fund-raising letter that claimed he'd won "special recognition" by *Chicago Magazine*. That magazine had called him one of the state's ten worst legislators. Another candidate who ran for election in a two-man race and lost made this upbeat concession statement: "I came in second, and my opponent came in next to last!"

In his earlier days, Rep. James Trificante, Jr. (D-Ohio) like most politicians in congress, held a local office. One of his opponents, a local sheriff, once claimed he was not rowing with both oars in the water. Trificante underwent an examination by a psychiatrist to assess his sanity. He passed the test and now brags that he is the only congressman who has been certified to be sane. While this tactic comes with certain risks, it most surely qualifies as making lemonade from lemons.

Enhance your image

Everybody can enhance their image with the appropriate humor. Even cops. A very popular Carlsbad, California, policeman used humor in this fashion. When he died at the age of thirty, twelve hundred people attended his funeral.

They recalled how the frame around his police motorcycle license plate read, "One more ticket and I get the microwave." (The humor here probably escaped those he ticketed.)

Humor columnist Dave Barry was writing an article about the shape of the human heart, which is not shaped like a valentine at all. He discovered that the only human organ with that configuration is the prostate gland. He then contacted the Hallmark Greeting Card Company to get their reaction and jokingly asked if this would precipitate their recall of the many greeting cards featuring the traditional heart shape. As befitting such a firm, their spokesperson conceded the point and responded that they had decided to sacrifice accuracy for sales after the poor performance of the following verse:

"Valentine, I'd follow you clear cross state,
For you to hold the key to my prostate."

Whether you want to build the image of your product, service, or yourself, remember that nothing will do that like a good dose of humor. Apply the humor solution and then sit back and watch it work for you.

"The best humor belongs to the person who can laugh at himself."
—Anon.

Chapter Two

Raise Your Humor Quotient

*"A genuine sense of humor is the pole that adds balance
to our steps as we walk the tightrope of life."*

—Anon.

What is a sense of humor? My definition of this sixth sense is being able to think funny *and* laugh at yourself. You'll find lots of people who can do one but not the other. You might say they have *half*-developed their sense of humor. This is important because when you put your sense of humor to work, it is usually in a situation where it happens automatically. That is, you just naturally use it without any forethought.

If you have a high humor quotient (H.Q.) you probably you probably got it from parents, other caretakers or a group of friends who also had this well-developed trait. Humor is acquired through osmosis. But besides hanging out with people with a good sense of humor, there are several things you can do to strengthen your own. Enhancing your sense of humor is not only fun but one of the best investments of your time you can make. Developing the ability to think funny and laugh in the face of adversity is a valuable asset you will cherish.

A sense of humor tends to automatically manifest itself in inauspicious situations, as when actress Carol Burnett got out of a taxi and caught her dress in the door. The driver, unaware of her plight, slowly began to make his way back into traffic. To keep from being yanked off her feet, the comedienne had to run alongside the cab. A passerby noticed her situation and alerted the driver. He stopped, jumped out and opened the door releasing her coat. Then he asked, "Are you all right?" Replied Carol Burnett, "Yes, but how much more do I owe you?"

"Every time we laugh at our own stupid selves, we reinforce our feelings for the ludicrous. We reinforce and expand it in its most essential realm, for we remind ourselves that foolishness, like charity, begins at home."
—Harvey Mindess

In such situations, you either think funny or you don't. This is probably why they say that humor acts as the springs of a vehicle as you travel down the rocky road of life. In humor workshops I've held, we do an interesting exercise. I ask the audience how many of them have a sense of humor. Virtually all hands go up every time. Everybody believes they have a sense of humor. They will agree to being everything from stupid to ugly before they will admit to being without one. Since my question is usually posed to people who work together and know each other quite well, it is always amusing to see how they look around at each other wondering why some of their co-workers have their hands up.

"In every real man a child is hidden who wants to play"
—Friedrich Nietzsche

Albert Schweitzer said that the tragedy of humankind is not that we die, but what dies within us while we live. What dies within most of us is the child we once were. That child had a sense of wonderment, a sense of playfulness and spontaneity that led to seeing the world through glasses tinted with humor. Studies show that the normal five-year-old laughs an average of 300 times a day. The average adult, on the other hand, laughs only fifteen times a day. It's healthy in many ways to keep the child alive. It dies within most of us as we make the transition to maturity. Life becomes very serious and we lose our ability to let go of the solemnity and laugh openly. This may be the result of too many admonitions from parents and teachers such as, "Wipe that silly smile off your face!"

It is worthwhile to work at keeping the child alive and vibrant. For a small percentage of people, the child within is alive and well and keeping it that way seems effortless. Others need to awaken the dormant child by consciously engaging in childlike activities. The creative/humorous mind is like a muscle.

If you use it, it will get stronger. Lets look at some ways of flexing our funny muscles.

Keeping the child alive

A colleague of mine who is a highly paid professional speaker actually walks through airports and other public places with the rolls from toilet paper on both feet. This may seem infantile but these kinds of zany activities truly enhance and hone one's sense of humor. They activate your dormant child and help to overcome the inhibitions that prevent us from taking the risks inherent in displaying a sense of humor. Sigmund Freud believed that humor and joking may be expressions of a person's attempt to return to the carefree days of childhood.

Here are some rather silly but effective exercises involving some healthy, good-natured practical joking that will help tickle your sense of humor and are also excellent for relieving stress.

- Call up friends to simply tell them a joke. You'll find they'll soon begin responding in kind.

- Send your doctor a bill for time spent in his waiting room.

- Leaf through *National Geographic* and draw underwear on the scantily-clad indigenous peoples of third world countries (AKA natives).

- Walk your cat on a leash.

Elevators are a great venue for fun and foolishness. They provide a captive audience you're not likely to see again. Thus, you can develop and practice your humor skills — especially those related to practical joking — in a relatively safe environment and have a lot of fun in the process. Comic genius Jonathan Winters and his pal Pat McCormick were well known for practical joking and their favorite place for this was the elevator. They would enter an elevator and pretend they had held up the office they just left. "Do you think we tied him up too tight," one would ask the other, pretending to be oblivious to their fellow passengers. One of their more outrageous pranks involved a visit to a butcher shop where they purchased tongue and other of the less popular cuts. Then they would put all this in a bucket and get on a hospital elevator dressed like doctors. There, they would engage in dialogue pretending they had just botched an operation. You can imagine the reaction of the others on the elevator.

Elevators are very good places to develop your practical joking skills.

Try these:

- Get on and face the rear.

- Peek into a slight opening of your purse or briefcase and say, "Got enough air in there?"

- After a passenger gets off, say to the remaining group, "I don't know about you folks, but I already miss him."

- Listen to the elevator walls with a stethoscope or start adding up the weight of the passengers and subtracting it from the limits posted on the sign.

More constructive frivolity:

- My 87-year-old father has a cap that reads, "Dirty old men need love too!" He wears it to the supermarket and tells me he always gets a kick out of watching the reactions of checkout people.

Try something like this or:

- Make up a silly poem or greeting card.

- Recall and share the most embarrassing thing that ever happened to you.

- Wear something outrageous — just for the heck of it.

- Buy a funny T-shirt. My favorite is, "Beer, it's not just for breakfast any more!"

- Celebrate an unusual occasion. Throw a party for Groundhog Day or . . .

- Start a humor file of cartoons and jokes.

Subscribe to a joke service. It will serve not only as a source of material but will be a regular stimulator for your humor quotient. Some feature timely comedy. One of the best is *Orben's Current Comedy* (P.O. Box 1992, Wilmington, DE 19899). It is used by professional speakers and writers. Remember, you get back what you put out. If you put humor out there, you'll get it back.

An acquaintance of mine goes into the men's room stalls and pulls out the paper toilet-seat cover. Then he writes on it with a marker pen: "Help, I'm stuck in here!" He tucks it back into the dispenser for the next guy to pull out. I save the messages from fortune cookies when I eat Chinese and then place them in the coin return slots of pay telephones for people to discover when they invariable search for leftover change. I even make up a few of my own. (e.g., "Don't stand still for long periods as pigeons mistake you for a statue.") The more outrageous your exercise, the more it improves your humor quotient.

> *"He deserves Paradise who makes his companions laugh"*
> —Mohammed, The *Koran*

Only people laugh because only people know what *ought* to be. Humor is a way of looking at the world. Much humor is spontaneous, unplanned and unexpected. A recent episode of the popular television program *60 Minutes* featured a story about a man who organizes efforts in states around the country to fight gambling. During the story, the day's winning California Lottery number flashed along the bottom of the screen.

Expose yourself to humor

I recently saw a sign at the zoo that read: "NO ANIMALS ALLOWED!" I'm sure the humor in this sign is unintentional and completely missed by the folks who run the zoo. Of course, there are many intentionally humorous signs that you'll see posted and will provide a chuckle. Here are a couple:

- God, grant me patience and I want it right now!

- Support mental health or I'll kill you!

Peruse newspapers and magazines for funny people such as Dave Barry. There may be others you like more. You may not even find Barry funny at all. That's okay. We all have slightly different ways to tickle our sixth sense. The point is to use it. Not everyone who goes to a gym works out the same way. Everybody does it a little differently, but exercise works for those who do it.

You are what you read

Newspapers offer two different ways to stimulate your humor quotient. One is the news which is centered on humorous events and the other is humorous columnists. I happen to think Dave Barry is tops as a humor writer. What is so funny is not necessarily his main premise, but rather the way he describes and relates them. Here is a quick blurb describing childbirth from an interview he did with *Playboy* magazine:

"Well, first of all, there are two systems for childbirth. There's the old system, under which I was born, where the man did not have to watch. That was a *good* system. The man's function was to sit in the waiting room and read old copies of *Field & Stream* and smoke a lot of Camels. As for the woman, she *did* have to be in the delivery room — you understand that part, right? — but she was given extensive narcotics and didn't wake up until the child was entering about the third grade." He goes on to discuss the birth of their only child, "So when the great day came and the baby was actually coming out, Beth was making noises like a whale, and she tried the breathing exercises and they were really effective for, oh, I'd say fifteen, possibly twenty seconds. Then she switched to the more traditional method, which is screaming for drugs."

The preceding is from an interview so I assume he had little time to dream up these narrations. It appears to me that he simply *thinks funny* in a way that I very much envy. Whether he is actually funny in his real life I do not know. I do know that many of the big-name comedians and humorists are totally devoid of humor in their personal lives. A number of them are known to be curmudgeons. So you can't assume, as most people do, that the stage persona you see is the real person. Rodney Dangerfield says, "People think comedians are happy. It's the reverse. When I was writing jokes at the age of fifteen, it wasn't because I was happy. It was to escape my reality." Some professionals use humor to escape or cope with reality. It is actually an excellent way to deal with life's unpleasantness.

Try to cultivate friendships with people who have this valuable trait. This is a chicken and egg situation. You acquire and keep friends with your sense of humor; but it is enhanced by these very same people.

Watch some of the many and varied funny television shows. Tape them if you have trouble being there for your favorites. Several humorous speakers I know tape both the David Letterman and Jay Leno monologues each weekday evening and then try to anticipate their topics (usually current items from the news) and treatment of them. This is a method of stimulating your own humorous outlook on current events.

Lucille Ball was one of the best comediennes ever and probably the most popular woman in the history of show business. She claimed her secret was to take everyday things and exaggerate them to the point of happy hysteria. She said she picked up the mechanics of comedy by osmosis, on radio and movie lots working with Bob Hope, Bert Lahr and the Marx Brothers. Osmosis is how all of us acquire this valued trait. That's why these exercises will work!

Humor is the convergence of dissimilar thought. It has been described as a "train wreck of the mind." A sign that reads "Croissants and Fill Dirt" is funny because you wouldn't expect to find both these items for sale in the same place. There is a cartoon of a fellow entering a room. The sign on the door reads, "Assertiveness Training — Barge Right In." This is congruent but funny. Humor is the association of things.

Finding your own humor

Write a joke a day. Use the matrix worksheet on page 30 for developing a joke. The matrix can be used to list disparate ideas and see their association in juxtaposition. You will see the connections that create humor. The worksheet should be enlarged and reproduced on a regular sheet of paper with several copies made for use the next time you want to create humor. Work the sheet and do similar exercises in your mind. Look out the window and think — associate and exaggerate; fuse disparate words, objects, services, trends and ambiances.

Check out the sample sheet on page 31 where the topic is flying. Maybe you'll come up with some ideas for a no-frills airline:

- that has coin-operated oxygen masks.

- where the passengers take turns blowing into the air supply.

- where there are no meals. Everyone is asked to bring a covered dish.

- that has no movies. The copilot passes around pictures of his vacation.

Mel Brooks was once asked where he got his humor. He replied that humor abounds in our lives if we just use our powers of observation. David Brinkley pointed out the government regulation that requires paint cans to bear a label reading, "Do Not Drink Paint." I had always wondered about the source of these silly admonitions on product labels. Drain cleaners carry this same caveat. As though we are going to down a glass of Draino when we're thirsty or if we have a sore throat. Mildew removal cautions us to use it only in "dry and well ventilated places." If it were dry and well ventilated, we wouldn't need the product! I recently bought a new VCR. It had a warning not to place it in water. Would someone actually take it home and put it in a pan of water?

"Wit consists in knowing the resemblance of things that differ and the difference of things that are alike."
—Germaine de Stael

Noticing funny things — whether they are the amusing use of words or something else — is really the essence of humor. Comedian Bobby Slayton observes that the musical *West Side Story* is ridiculous. A guy comes into an Hispanic neighborhood, hollers "Maria" and only one woman comes to the window!

George Carlin is amazed by Thanksgiving. On that day modern life is demonstrated in homes all over the country as millions of turkeys baste themselves in millions of ovens that clean themselves. Humor emerges from the ability to see the follies of our times.

National events and trends tend to make for some propitious humor. Major cities around the country all seem to be vying for major league sports teams. Football and baseball in particular are the big prizes. As cities scramble to lure these teams from other cities there is a lot of municipal stress. Fortunately, there has been room for a little humor too. Citizens have suggested such team names as the Buffalo Chips, the District of Columbia Tricky Dickies and the Tampa Bay Polidents. The advent of the impotency pill, Viagra, has spawned a plethora of such jokes: "St. Petersburg, Florida, being renamed Viagra Falls."

Everyday events lend themselves to such humorous scrutiny:

- Nothing is more satisfying than parking on someone else's remaining parking meter time.

- If God had meant for us to travel tourist class, he would have made us narrower.

- We're all self-made but only the rich will admit it.

Often, euphemisms used seriously provide hilarious results. Harris Bank of Chicago said it was "rightsizing the bank," which, it explained, meant reduction of "payroll costs through reducing head count." Similarly, a Vermont company gave fifteen employees the heave-ho after its president explained that the action was not really a layoff or cutback but "a career-change opportunity." The *Wall Street Journal* refers to workers who have been laid off as "redundant," "excessed," "transitioned" or workers offered "voluntary severance." So, if you're on the way out, don't expect your boss to come right out and say it. Look for a fancy euphemism.

Nearly every occupation has its own set of slang. In the medical field, for example, we find that "gone camping" describes a patient in an oxygen tent. A "blue pipe" is a vein, a "red pipe" is an artery and a "wig picker" is the same as a "shrink." Newspapers and other periodicals often contain unintentionally hilarious items. Here is a correction notice from a newsletter: "Mai Thai is one of the students in the program and was in the center of the photo. We incorrectly listed her as one of the items on the menu." And this item from the *New Zealand Times*: "The horse is an 8-year-old gelding trained by the owner who races him with his wife."

A great many knowledgeable people have observed from time to time that analyzing humor is like inspecting frog gizzards — the only way to accomplish your goal is to kill your subject. Nevertheless, it's nice to have just a little insight into what makes comedy work.

> *"There are three rules for creating humor,*
> *but unfortunately no one knows what they are."*
> —Laurence Peter

Here are just a few rules and guidelines on the subject. Nothing is funny to anybody unless they can relate to it. There is the joke about a guy who keeps going to confession for stealing. After two of these sessions (jokes are always set up in three parts with the last one fodder for the punch line) the priest tells him to make a novena. He says, "OK father, if you've got the plans, I'll get the lumber." The joke is only funny if you know what a novena is. It would go over well with a Catholic group but any other audience it would be left cold.

I once attended a luncheon where Henny Youngman was the speaker/comic. The event was in Miami Beach and he apparently thought the audience was Jewish. So his jokes were Jewish with Yiddish punch lines. The audience was

	RELATED	UNRELATED	
WORDS, PHRASES & CLICHÉS			TOPIC=
EVENTS			
THINGS			
PLACES			
PEOPLE			

	PEOPLE	PLACES	THINGS	EVENTS	WORDS, PHRASES & CLICHÉS
RELATED	PILOTS PASSENGERS FLIGHT ATTENDANTS GROUND CREW AIR TRAFFIC CONTROLLERS TRAVEL AGENTS	AIRPORTS PARKING LOTS AIRPORT BARS RESTAURANTS FAST FOOD PODIUMS RUNWAYS TARMACK	AIRPLANES SEATS MEALS/FOOD TICKETS FIRST CLASS BARF BAGS MAGAZINES OXYGEN MASKS AIR BLOWERS SEAT BELTS EMERGENCY EXITS	LOST BAGGAGE LATE FLIGHTS SAFETY LECTURE SEATING AIR FARE WARS TOURS CRASHES TAKE-OFFS LANDINGS MOVIES	WELCOME TO... "FINAL DESTINATION" SAFETY RESERVATIONS OVER BOOKINGS SWA - NO FRILLS UFK/O'HARE/DULLES AIRLINES CHEAP FLIGHT TRAVEL
UNRELATED	BUS DRIVERS TRAIN CONDUCTORS CHAUFFEURS HIGHWAY DRIVERS	HIGHWAYS ROADS STREETS BUS STATIONS RAILROAD TERMINALS	TRAINS CARS BUSES SUBWAYS TRAIN FOOD FOREIGN AIRLINES LIMOUSINES	SALES TRAIN STOPS	UNNOTICED ARRIVAL STAY AT HOME GREYHOUND BUS CO.

full of Gentiles and nobody seemed to know what was going on. Of course, Youngman quickly picked up on it and made the necessary adjustment.

Having fun with words

Sometimes words are paired up or strung together in peculiar ways. Robert Klien discusses food labels that advise us the products contain "an acceptable level of rodent hairs. There is *no level* of this stuff that is acceptable to me!"

George Carlin is amused by the term "legally drunk." "Officer, leave him alone. He's *legally* drunk!"

People such as Yogi Berra, Casey Stengel and movie producer Samuel Goldwyn were known for, among other things, their convoluted language. Stengel once said, "Everybody line up in alphabetical order, according to your size." Berra had many of these classics including, "Baseball is ninety percent mental. The other half is physical." On another occasion he explained why he bought an expensive life insurance policy: "I'll get it when I die."

> *"Only if we are secure in our beliefs*
> *can we see the comical side of the universe."*
> —Flannery O'Connor

Goldwyn seems to have been the undisputed king of these illogical phrases. Among the gems attributed to him: "If I could drop dead right now, I'd be the happiest man alive," and, "An oral contract isn't worth the paper it's written on." Berra and Goldwyn were thought to have uttered these contradictions inadvertently. Leo Rosten also had a reputation for uttering such nonsense but most believed he did it intentionally. He reportedly said about one of his friends, "He gets up a six o'clock in the morning no matter what time it is."

Staying clear of puns

Secretary of the Department of Energy, Frederico Peña, announced new efficiency rules for refrigerator manufacturers by saying, "Not to steal from the president, but we're building a fridge for the 21st century." This was a play on the president's slogan for his reelection: "Building a bridge to the 21st century." This pun (play on words) worked because of Peña's stature as a member of the president's cabinet and because the humor was somewhat self-directed. It is a good idea, however, to stay away from using puns. They might work on rare occasions — usually one-on-one with friends, but they will nearly always evoke groans from a larger audience. Puns are considered the opposite of self-deprecating humor. They convey the unspoken message: *Look how smart I am!*

An exception seems to be the use of what appears to be an unintentional pun, followed by the comment, "No pun intended."

If you're into the humor of language you might want to participate or at least observe the program of Lake Superior State University in Sault Ste. Marie, Michigan 49783. They collect and disseminate funny words on an annual basis. They publish posters and a yearly calendar with ridiculous euphemisms and words they consider redundant or misused. George Carlin claims that environmentalists changed their terminology to *rain forests* and *wetlands* because no one would give them money to save *jungles* and *swamps*.

> *"Comedy is a distraction, not an action. Humor takes your mind off the negative and turns it into laughter that's positive."*
> —Buddy Hackett

Jokes are an important way to keep humor in your life. But there is much more to humor than simply remembering jokes and retelling them. Here are just a few tips about jokes: Jokes are normally comprised of characters, setting and theme. You can often easily switch the first two. For example: "The post office has announced they are going to shorten their lines. Everybody is going to stand closer together." The subject or theme is lines. The setting is the post office. There are no characters. The joke can be switched to such places as the Department of Motor Vehicles, the local supermarket or any locale that typically has lines. Switching can be used to tailor the joke to your audience as well as make an old joke new by changing the characters, setting or theme. Ethnic jokes are a good example. Many of them began life as moron jokes and then became Polish jokes and so on. Most ethnic jokes can be switched to key on occupations, religions or avocations.

Punch lines and punch words

Jokes are comprised of a setup and a punch line. Punch lines contain what is called a "punch word." That is the word that makes the joke work. It should always be placed as close to the end of the punch line as possible. Ideally, it is the last word, but that cannot always be worked out. Here's a joke: A motorist, after being bogged down in a muddy road, paid a passing farmer $20 to pull him out with his tractor. After he was back on dry ground, he said to the farmer, "At those prices, I should think you would be pulling people out of the mud night and day." The farmer said, "I can't, 'cause I haul water for that hole at night." The punch word, the word that makes the joke work, is water. Thus, the punch line should be rearranged: " I can't, cause at night I haul water for that hole."

The punch word is moved more toward the end of the punch line, making the joke more effective. The punch word should also be emphasized.

> *"A man with a sense of humor doesn't make jokes out of life;*
> *he merely recognizes the ones that are there."*

—Anon.

When you've heard the joke before, don't stop the teller. This is an opportunity to hone your joke-telling skills. Since you've heard the joke, pay attention to the delivery. Are the words descriptive? Is suspense being built up? Does the teller pause before delivering the punch line? What is the punch word? Is it at the end of the punch line? Was it emphasized? These are the dynamics that make a joke well-told.

Humor should be unexpected. Sneak up on them. Never telegraph the fact that you are going to tell a joke. It's always funnier if they're not expecting it. Also, if you can see the punch line coming, it won't have the effect you want. It should sneak up on them too.

One of the most valuable properties of humor is that it makes people think. A thought stated too succinctly is not funny. Effective humor always evokes the *ah ha factor*. A joke or one-liner must be presented in such a way that the recipient must process the information for the "ah ha" in it.

To see the ah ha factor at work, try this: Go up to a friend and, with a straight face, acting very sincere, tell them you like an item of clothing and ask them if they "bought it new." As in, "Say Fred, I've been admiring your sport coat. Did you buy that new?" Then watch their face as they process the question. You'll see them accept it and as they think about the answer, the alternative thought (that they might have purchased it used) will occur and generate the humor. You will actually witness the ah ha factor at work.

You can sit and lecture a youngster about the value of education. Or, you can tell the same youngster that the amount of education he gets will determine whether he showers *before* he goes to work or *after*. The latter will cause him to think about the point and to subsequently "get it."

The point of the joke should be indirect. The listener must have to *think* to get it. Here's another farmer joke to illustrate the point: On a drive in the country, a city slicker noticed a farmer lifting his pig up to an apple tree and holding it there as it ate one apple after another. The farmer repeated this with a second and then a third pig. The city fellow went up to the farmer and said, "Wouldn't it save a lot of time if you just shook the tree so the apples fell to the ground?" "Time?" said the farmer. "What does time matter to a pig?"

To see the importance of the indirect nature of humor, let's dissect a joke: God telephones the Pope and says to him, "Pope, I've got good news and I've got bad news. The good news is I've come back to earth and I've decided to unify all the religions of the world. The bad news is I'm calling you from Salt Lake City."

If, instead of this punchline, God were to say (direct), "I've decided on Mormonism," it wouldn't be funny. The fact that you must make that conclusion yourself by extrapolating Salt Lake City (indirect) is what gives the joke its humor.

Personalizing the quip

Remember the ROI or *return on investment* rule. It dictates that the enjoyment produced by the joke should compensate the audience for the time spent listening to it. An aside, for example, does not require laughter, whereas a joke with a setup, should reap a suitable period of appreciation. What is suitable depends on the length of the joke or the amount of the listener's time you've taken.

A joke or quip can be made funnier by personalizing it. Instead of saying, "These two guys were in a supermarket," say, "Jim and I were in Krogers." Mentioning specific people and places helps people visualize the setting and adds to the setup of the joke. In joke telling, the idea is to create a picture in the mind of the listener. Act out your humor when possible.

You've probably noticed comedians always "act it out." It adds to the delivery. Don't be afraid to exaggerate. If the story calls for outrage, for example, throw your arms up in the air or clench your fists and place them on your hips. If a look of puzzlement is appropriate, squint your eyes and scratch your head. Add voice modulation. Consider this joke: Three guys are interviewing for an accounting position. The CEO asks the first, "How much is two and two?" "Four," he replies. The second applicant is asked the same question and gives the same answer. When the question is put to the third and successful candidate, he leans forward, looks around, and whispers, "How much do you *want* it to be?" Imagine how much more effective this story is when you actually lean forward, look around and whisper the punch line.

> *"Angels can fly because they take themselves lightly"*
>
> —Anon.

Here are few basics related to using all humor: It should meet the AT&T test. That is, it should be *appropriate, timely* and *tasteful*. If it is, it should not

35

backfire. If it does not meet all three of these criteria, it is likely to get a groan or perhaps be received negatively.

Appropriate: The humor should fit the occasion and the audience. What goes over at a bowling banquet might not be appropriate at a religious gathering. There is much subjectivity here so it has to be left to the individual to judge appropriateness.

Timely: You might remember several years ago when there were a couple of shootings at post offices in different parts of the country. I was emceeing a program at about that time and, without thinking about the timeliness of it, used a joke about the post office. It didn't go over. Later, when I thought about the reason, I realized it was because the joke was not timely.

Tasteful: This is even more subjective than appropriateness. Again, what is tasteful depends on the audience, occasion and general community standards. The real key is knowing your audience — because, after all, it is *their* taste that is the determinant.

One key factor in the AT&T test is the person actually telling the joke. An African-American can tell a joke about African-Americans, but a white person telling the same joke is on shaky ground. Cartoonist John Callahan does drawings of handicapped people in comic settings. He could not even begin to get away with that if he were not handicapped himself. Even so, he get lots of criticism. On the other hand, he gets plaudits from many handicapped folks.

You can't always know the group experiences of the audience. You may be doing a joke about death in front of people who have recently lost a colleague. If so, you might get bushwhacked and that is why humor is always risky. Evaluations for appropriateness and tastefulness are somewhat subjective. The monologist must always be aware he is walking a fine line that divides irreverence from bad taste. On the other hand, if you choose to omit everything with negative connotations, you'll have little material left. Subject matter with a little bite gets bigger laughs but one must be aware of where to draw the line. For instance, former Vice-president Dan Quayle was fair game for his duffer image, but former Senator Wilbur Mills became off-limits when it was discovered he was an alcoholic.

"A person reveals his character by nothing so clearly as the joke he resents."
—G.C. Lichtenberg

Humor and laughter are contagious. The fact that laughter is contagious is the reason behind the use of laugh tracks on television sit-coms. Humor's contagiousness can be seen in the fact that when one person tells a joke, invariably, someone else will tell a joke. People will usually laugh when laughter is expected. That's why a below-standard routine in comedy clubs gets more laughs than it deserves. People in the audience came to laugh and know they are supposed to find the material funny.

Experiments have been done where a top comedian would tell a few regular jokes and then tell one but leave out the punch line. In these cases, laughter flowed just as if the punch line had been delivered. Al Jolson once experimented with this by telling four continuous jokes without punch lines and got four good laughs.

A little bit about humor and laughter

Someone once asked Charlie Chaplin to explain comedy. "Why," they asked, "do people find humor in a man walking down the street and slipping on a banana peel?" Chaplin reportedly said, "That is not funny. What is funny is a guy walking down the street and jumping over a banana peel and landing in an open manhole!"

Cartoonist Al Capp, creator of *Li'l Abner* and *Fearless Fosdick*, had his own example. "A snooty, rich, fat lady slipping on the sidewalk and skinning her knee isn't funny. But if the same lady falls head over heels down a full flight of stairs and winds up with her head in a goldfish bowl, that's funny."

Humor is surprise and incongruity. A store sign advertising sushi and fish bait is funny because the items are similar as well as incongruent. It is the clash of two actions or ideas that don't really fit together. When the rule of three is used for jokes (as it almost always is) the third one is incompatible and conflicts with the previous two. The incongruity must ring true and is even funnier if it is emotionally charged. This juxtaposition — the fact that you expect one thing and get another — is the essence of humor. Someone once defined humor as "a train wreck of the mind."

> "Incongruity is the mainspring of laughter."
> —Max Beerbohm

The humor of overstatement and understatement is only funny if there is at least a kernel of truth in it. Without some truth, it won't be funny. Aristotle wrote that humor is the pleasurable distortion of what is expected. Sid Caesar says that comedy has to be truth. "You take the truth and you put a little curlicue at the end." It is important to keep in mind that truth is a very personal thing, based on experiences, intelligence and outlook on life. For something to be funny it has to relate to our sense of these things. We are all the center of our own universe. People driving slower than us on the freeway are "poking around" while those going faster are "maniacs." That is the nature of humankind. If you believe that you are perfectly normal, keep in mind the axiom that *everybody is somebody else's weirdo*.

Misunderstanding and humor

Misunderstandings make excellent grist for the humor mill. Many jokes are based on that theme. But real-life misunderstandings are even funnier. I once worked for a credit and bill collection agency in Ohio. The name of the firm was the North Canton Collection Agency. One day a woman called to ask about our charges. She had seen the company's name and assumed it was a *garbage* collection service. Of course I didn't know that and provided her with our costs which were contingency fees of thirty-three and fifty percent, depending on the amount involved and method of collection.

Looking back on our conversation, it was hilarious, as you might imagine. When I told the woman our charge was a percentage, she asked, "A percentage of what?" When I answered, "The amount we collect," she said, "Well you can keep it all!" It was only when I discovered that she thought we would be collecting trash instead of money from past due accounts, that I envisioned her imagining us going through her garbage to determine which items we wished to retain.

When trombonist Fu Min Huang of the United States International University orchestra was to marry, a group of Chinese students was invited to the wedding shower. Two of them showed up with towels believing they had been invited to join the bride in some bizarre Western custom of showering with her.

Many jokes are based on misunderstandings and misinterpretations. Here's an example: The doctor finished his examination of the patient and said, "I just can't find a cause for your illness. Frankly, I think it's due to drinking."

"In that case," replied the patient, "I'll come back when you're sober."

Playing off current events and trends

Reading joke books is a good way to enhance your sixth sense, relieve stress and gather some valuable material at the same time. But you don't read a joke book the same way you read a regular book. Read it in less than twenty minute segments. After fifteen minutes or so, they become tiresome and the humor becomes elusive. As you read these collections, take a moment to examine them for the joke-telling criteria mentioned above.

You'll probably recall the bumper stickers popular a number of years ago that read, "Baby On Board." These spawned a plethora of humorous off-shoots such as "Mother-in-Law in Trunk."

More recently, bumper stickers began appearing with the message:

"MY CHILD WAS STUDENT OF THE MONTH
AT ST. GEORGE PRE-SCHOOL"

This brought forth responses such as:

"MY UNCLE IS A TRUSTEE AT THE DOWNTOWN JAIL"

and:

"MY BROTHER-IN-LAW WAS INMATE OF THE MONTH AT
DONOVAN CORRECTIONAL INSTITUTION"

Finally, stickers began showing up that read:

"MY KID BEAT THE HELL OUT OF THE CITIZEN OF THE
MONTH AT SOUTH BAY HIGH SCHOOL"

Humor tends to spring up to meet fads and trends and then begets itself. There is ubiquitous evidence of the public's sense of humor. When the Pittsburgh Steelers were preparing to go to the Super Bowl, even the prisoners at the local county jail got behind them. A black and gold sign was strung outside the building reading, "GO STEALERS."

Signs are a good way to surround yourself with humor and signal your H.Q. Here is a sign I like:

"WHEN I DIE,
I'D LIKE TO GO PEACEFULLY IN MY SLEEP
LIKE MY GRANDFATHER,
NOT YELLING AND SCREAMING
LIKE THE PASSENGERS IN HIS CAR."

Someone once said that most jokes are about death and sex because those are the two things we are most anxious about. Air travel tends to generate a lot of humor, probably because there is so much anxiety related to it. Comedian George Carlin has a very funny routine about the so-called safety lecture we get upon takeoff. He also has fun with the announcement by the stewardess welcoming the passengers to the city where they've just landed. "Who is she to welcome us?" asks Carlin, "the Mayor's wife?"

Pretensions are always fine targets for humor. Letting the air out of the balloon tires of pomposity is a surefire formula for some frivolity. In the comic pages of yesteryear there were many cartoons featuring snowballs being thrown at top hats. This is an example of pomposity as a target. From time to time, the populace seems to go either toward or away from a collective sense of humor.

The American public has become so uptight that many are joining the ranks of the humor-impaired. Rush Limbaugh, whose appeal is primarily to ultra-conservatives, recently played a joke on his radio audience. During the UPS strike by the Teamsters Union, Limbaugh read a fake fax that was supposed to be from UPS management stating that if the strikers persisted, the company was going to export many of the jobs to Guatemala. Many listeners took it seriously. The story even spilled over to other media. If anyone had bothered to take a moment they would have realized that a worker in Guatemala could not very well deliver a package in Des Moines. The ludicrousness escaped many people.

The plague of political correctness

I believe I'm typical of most people in the humor profession in that I decry the advent of "political correctness." It has diminished the opportunities for tasteful humor by imposing a new, strict and artificial standard for what is acceptable. Humor is a way of looking at the world. By its very nature it is irreverent and iconoclastic. That is to say that when we see something that is incongruent or seems ironic, we exaggerate to illuminate it even more. This is a method of developing humor. "P.C." limits the material available. The movement has even taken its toll on the funny pages. Traditional comic strips are under attack because some group somewhere is offended. There was even a movement to suppress the recent Disney movie about Mr. Magoo, the nearsighted, ill-tempered and incompetent cartoon character. It seems that "sight challenged" people had taken offense.

On Thanksgiving Day, 1997, the nineteen-year tradition of the Turkey Olympics in Warren, Connecticut, died in a head-on collision with P.C. The event previously attracted about 1,000 people who watched turkeys compete in athletic events and beauty contests. The previous year's winner was a turkey wearing a fur coat and pearls named "Gretta Gobble" (after the reclusive 1930s film star). Even though the turkeys were not harmed in any way, animal rights protesters created a safety problem that prompted cancellation of the competition.

> *"You can discover more about a person in an hour of play*
> *than in a year of conversation."*
> —Plato

I predict that this P.C. thing will run its course and after being carried to its extreme will fade out. People will get sick of it when they see it for what it is. Lighten up America! Recently the city of Dickson, N.D., rejected P.C. and went on the offensive. The local high school's nickname was the Midgets — depicted by a squat, frowning boy. The name was coined in the 1920s in honor of the school's short but scrappy basketball players. School board members said the image and nickname were inappropriate and insensitive and moved to change it — after seventy years of tradition. By an overwhelming vote, the townspeople restored the name and mascot, then canned the board members who had voted to dump it.

I do comedy roasts and also serve as an advisor to others planning such events. The first series of questions I ask a client is about the target of the proposed roast. I explain that a roast is a verbal caricature of the roastee. That is, you take his or her physical, social, political and other characteristics and play off of them. Frequently, I'll be told such things as, "Well he's bald but don't make a joke of it because he's very sensitive. And he's been married several times but don't say anything about that." What we have here is an unroastable character. He's got the characteristics for a good roast but he's too sensitive to have any fun with them. Political correctness is analogous to this situation. We can't joke about this and we can't laugh about that because people are sensitive and they'll take offense. As a result, our potential subject matter is being diminished faster than the ozone layer.

Real humor is thinking funny

While we're on the subject of chiding humor I'd like to relate an interesting observation I've made. I conduct a fascinating exercise in my humor workshops. I ask the attendees how many of them enjoy the humor of Rodney Dangerfield. Then I ask how many like Don Rickles. Usually, this will dichotomize the audience. A few will like both but it usually breaks down that about sixty-five percent are fond of Dangerfield and the rest like Rickles. What is so interesting to me is that both men use the very same humor. In Dangerfield's case it is self-directed, while in Rickles' case, the opposite is true. You can usually take a joke from either one, reverse it and use it in the other's routine. Dangerfield may say, "I asked my girlfriend how, on a scale of one to ten, I rated as a lover. She asked me if I understood fractions." And Rickles would say, "He asked his wife . . . ."

My good friend Bob was stopped by the police and given a field sobriety test. The officer stood on one foot with his arms spread out in the air and told Bob to imitate his stance. My friend assumed the position beside him and, observing that they looked like a dance team said, "I think we could make it in Las Vegas! But I want top billing." Cops are not known for their sense of humor and this one was no different. But Bob got a big chuckle out of it, and, since he was stone sober, the policeman could do nothing but wonder what Bob found so amusing. Although the wittiest fellow I've ever known was a lawyer, it has been my experience that attorneys, doctors and police are the most humor-impaired occupations.

Humor attracts

One of the wonderful things about humor, fun and play is that people are unwittingly attracted to them. It's almost a human trait. Or perhaps it is a remedy for our times. Jim Nayder is an independent radio producer known for his dry sense of humor. When WBEZ-FM of Chicago asked him to fill a few moments on the air, his strange sense of the absurd surfaced. He came up with the most annoying song he could find. Listeners went for it big time! The telephone began ringing and people wanted to know when they could have an encore.

Annoying Music is now a weekly staple on the Chicago station and has been picked up by ninety public radio stations nationally. It's a brief three-minute segment, but immensely popular. His initial selection was a yodeling rendition of *It's a Small World*, followed by similar ditties. His method of selecting tunes for this hit show provides an interesting insight into such humor. He will not select a song that is intentionally bad or funny.

Minor-league fun

Minor-league baseball is not usually a profitable undertaking. It exists primarily to develop talent for the major leagues and is subsidized by them. Attendance is normally modest at these games, but Mike Veeck, owner of the St. Paul Saints, recognized the fertility of fun and decided to cash in on it. His Midway Stadium sells out of season tickets while just across the river, the major-league Minnesota Twins play to thousands of empty seats. His magic is in the mirth he injects. Every half-inning, some promotion is staged.

He has dressed men in rubber sumo wrestler suits (one representing the Saints and the other the opposing team) and have them go at it while the crowd cheers and boos. The team mascot is a pig named Tobias who is sometimes

dressed in a tutu. He delivers balls to home-plate via his saddlebag. Baseball became inordinately popular after Veeck made it fun through the use of humor and other theatrics. There are many other examples of the public's attraction to the humorously bizarre. Years ago, it was the emergence of pet rocks and such other weird fads.

A similar current item is "Boyfriend In-A-Box" for single women looking for the perfect man. It was invented by Cathy Hamilton who recently came up with the idea and, after failing to interest Hallmark Cards, decided to market it on her own. In the past eight months she has sold more than $40,000 worth at $16 each. They come in six models, the best selling of which are *Doctor Dave* and *Corporate Craig*. These boxed-up boyfriends come with photos of various sizes, a sheet of basic facts, an owner's manual, messages, greeting cards, a flower sender's card and other items they can strew around their desks. The Boyfriend-In-A-Box even comes with a warranty.

Humor is revealing

One of the great aspects of humor is that it is telling. Nothing is funny unless there is some element of truth in it. When someone is offended, it is often because the humor hit too close to home. People who cannot laugh at themselves are usually insecure. Humor has a way of disclosing personality quirks and strengths. It can also be used to uncover motives.

The late Earl Warren, while governor of California, arrived at work one morning accompanied by a friend. There were a number of men waiting for him in his outer office. Warren paused as he passed through and told them a very old joke. When they got into his office his friend commented on the joke. "That was a pretty old chestnut you pulled out there," he said.

"I know," replied Warren, "but I wanted to find out how many are here to ask favors."

His friend asked, "Well did you?"

"Oh yes," Warren said, "They were the ones who laughed."

Whatever your profession or occupation, working on increasing your H.Q. will pay dividends in many areas of your life. If you've developed "comic vision," you can call upon it to relax you — which will deal with stressful situations and help you perform better in just about any activity.

Chapter Three

Promote Your Product or Service

*"Humor is the lubrication oil of business.
It prevents friction and wins good will."*

—Anon.

Max Schling, a New York City florist, stimulated sales by running an ad in the *New York Times* entirely in shorthand. Curious executives had to ask their secretaries for a translation. The copy read, "Remember Schling when the boss needs flowers." When David Merrick produced *The Matchmaker* on Broadway, he bought an old English taxicab, with its high gates on either side, and had it transformed so it could be driven from the rear seat. A well-dressed fellow sat in the rear and, unnoticed, drove the car. In the front seat Merrick placed a chimpanzee in a chauffeur's cap, its hand strapped to a non-functioning steering wheel. A sign on the side of the cab read, "I'm driving my master to see *The Matchmaker*." The car was driven all around Times Square four or five times a day. Soon people were waiting in line to buy tickets.

In a promotional gimmick, a New York shoe company put shoes on the statue of Atlas in Rockefeller Center. It took six hours for security guards to get around to removing them. In the meantime, the stunt attracted the media and provided a bundle of free publicity. Be imaginative, nervy and don't be afraid to use some showbiz glitz. Humorous antics are one of the best ways to promote yourself, your product or your idea. You'll note that in the above cases there was a marriage between humor and theater. Showmanship is the key. Humorous thinking is the engine that can propel your promotional campaign.

During the hubbub around President Bill Clinton and his alleged paramour, Monica Lewinsky, Micron Electronics seized the moment with a clever idea. They sent out their latest press kit in an envelope made to look like it came from the White House. Looking very much like a continuous-use routing envelope, it was replete with phony dates, senders, receivers and departments as well as faked signatures. There were many humorous entries including one thanking the president for "the dress." It was enormously successful and was even reproduced in *Newsweek* magazine.

One of the all-time great promoters was P.T. Barnum. He used his sense of humor and theatrical genius to garner press for his cause and his entrepreneurship. To make sure people read his outdoor advertisements, he put them on the backs of signs that read, "Don't read the Other Side."

Bouncing back with humor

Barnum built a museum located near a church whose members opposed his shows and displays and wanted nothing to do with him. When P.T. wanted to celebrate the Fourth of July, he waited until nightfall and strung banners and pennants from his museum across the street to the only other building that would accommodate them — the church. When church officials objected, Barnum told them he would take them down but only in front of a photographer who would send pictures to newspapers of Old Glory being removed at the church's request on the Fourth of July. The banners remained and his museum experienced a record attendance.

Barnum lost his fortune three times because of fires that wiped him out. But each time he bounced back, using publicity and his entrepreneurial skills — based on humor and theater. Early in his career, he had a famous exhibit called "The Happy Family." It featured a lion, a tiger and a lamb living together in the same cage. When asked by a friend how long he expected to keep the attraction running, Barnum answered, "As long as the supply of lambs holds out." Incidentally, he never said, "There is a sucker born every minute."

The publishers of *New York* magazine got more attention than they had hoped for when they placed an ad on city buses that chided Mayor Rudy Giuliani. The advertisement called its magazine "possibly the only good thing in New York Rudy hasn't taken credit for." Histrionics gets attention, which is necessary to convey any message. The folks in Los Angeles were lobbying the NFL for a football team. So when the NFL owners met in San Diego in 1997, they had chef James Boyce deliver the owners an edible replica of the L.A. Coliseum on a mirrored plate with their message inscribed in chocolate: "Location is Everything — The Los Angeles Coliseum."

When the 1998 Super Bowl was held in San Diego, county officials jumped on this opportunity to try to entice corporations to move their headquarters to the area. But rather than employ the usual tactics they opted for some showbiz strategy. First, they had a photograph of county supervisors and their CEO taken against a sunny harbor skyline sporting dark suits and sunglasses — a business version of the Blues Brothers. They made this into a special greeting to CEOs slated to visit. As the VIPs arrived, county representatives greeted them at the airport with suntan lotion and a note that read, "Get some sun out of life — San Diego." They reported an enthusiastic response.

Humor spotlights

The point is if you really want to be noticed and remembered, do something different. Author Harvey Mackay tells how he once had the task of picking up television's Ted Koppel at the airport when he visited Minneapolis to give a speech. He found out that Ted was an avid tennis player and on the way in from the airport they stopped for a game of tennis. After Koppel returned home, Harvey sent him a note telling him how nice it was to have met him. Along with the note he sent a giant 35-inch tennis racquet and a tennis ball one hundred times the size of a regular one. Koppel is not likely to forget Mackay, who tells the story to make his point that doing it differently — and with some flair — is the way to go.

It is good to anticipate the various outcomes of your genius. Using innovative ideas brings to mind the story that George Burns used to tell about working in the garment district when he was young. Business was slow and Burns approached his boss with an idea. Why not send out thirteen dozen unrequested blouses to the town's merchants with a note referring to "twelve dozen." Burns reasoned they would recognize the error and keep them believing they had gotten a windfall. The boss, who was also the owner, liked the idea and implemented it. Later, when called into his office, Burns envisioned being offered a partnership. But, he said, that thought evaporated when he saw his boss's expression. The merchants had returned twelve of the thirteen dozen and kept the other one.

Humor is an excellent method of bringing positive attention to your product or idea. There are many ways to promote a product or service but a humorous approach is certainly among the most effective.

The Watergate Hotel, site of the infamous burglary, celebrated its thirtieth anniversary in June of 1997. Ironically, it was also the twenty-fifth anniversary of the break-in that served as the catalyst for Nixon's resignation. So they threw a champagne-sparkled banquet that featured waiters dressed as Secret Service agents and tables decorated with newsprint and shredded cassettes. They also offered "Break-In" packages which included souvenirs and memorabilia, and put together "Weekend Furlough" or "Executive Privilege" plans for guests.

When Madison Avenue brainstormed methods for promoting Avery Hi-Liter pens, they decided to take a cue from the previous year's trendy dance — the Macarena. The company announced it would send 22 neon-clad dancers into the streets of Chicago for two months to perform the "Avery Hi-Liter Dance." Traveling in a special neon-colored bus shaped like one of their pens, the dancers will, according to the announcement, wear vests adorned with pens of various colors, twirl batons and chant lines such as "Invented in '63' / Hi-Liter brand from Avery / Try it once and you'll be sold / With our new EverBold."

Even political parties engage in hoopla to capture the imagination of the public. Republicans kicked off a national campaign to scrap the current income tax code with a Capitol pep rally that featured "Scrap the Tax Tour" T-shirts, rock music and confetti made from torn-up income tax forms.

Skyrocketing sales

Promotion often involves drama. The more dramatic and the more humorous, the better. *Inside Media*, an industry newsletter, related a highlight from Joan Rivers' *Can We Shop* television shill show. A man was extolling the virtues of a new, revolutionary toilet bowl cleaner. It was a 50,000 flush, chemical free, bacteria-killing, mildew-destroying, environmentally safe product. To make his point, he had Joan Rivers spoon a glass of treated water right out of the toilet, then he gulped it down in front of the television audience. Sales of the product skyrocketed and the dramatic gulping ploy sold 5,100 units of the stuff at $19.95 each. Using current events is probably the most effective way to promote something because you leverage contemporary interest and publicity. When the movie *Dances With Wolves* was enjoying popularity in theaters, a Seattle seafood restaurant chain began airing a television commercial showing a Kevin Costner look-alike waltzing with giant shellfish.

Sometimes the product itself suggests a method of promotion based on its purpose. Blistex lip balm, for example, has been getting lots of free press for seventeen years now by choosing and publicizing lip-smacking champions from among the theatrical, political and athletic elite. Some categories: Most Phenomenal Lips, Most Twisted Lips, Most Dashing Lips, Most Talkative Lips and Most Overlooked Lips. Tying these celebrity types into its product with a humorous spin ballyhoos what would otherwise be a bland commodity into a more exciting one.

From about 1965 the California Raisin Growers saw sales of their product decline at one to two percent each year. Their advertising highlighted their slogan which was "a drop of sunshine in every raisin." Then, in 1987, they changed their promotional campaign to feature a group of dancing raisins bopping to the tune of Marvin Gaye's *I Heard it Through the Grapevine*. Chances are you've seen this commercial. It was enormously successful and sales jumped ten to twenty percent. In 1988, it captured the number one ranking for ad awareness. All the fun got people excited about these fruity little items. The ad grabbed viewers' attention and took them through the several steps from feeling good, to smiling, to connecting those feelings with raisins.

It is difficult to overstate the benefits of creating pleasant feelings. According to the *Wall Street Journal*, when the Bank of Ann Arbor promised it would pay buyers of a twelve-month certificate of deposit one-quarter of a percent more if Michigan beat Colorado in football, the offer attracted $3 million worth of sales in six weeks.

Many companies have found that humor imparts an image of vitality and the message that the company doesn't take itself too seriously, which reflects well on their product or service. Following his loss in the race for president in 1996, Bob Dole appeared in an Air France newspaper ad hawking low-priced airline tickets. Above a picture of him smiling and waving was a headline that read, "Not doing anything? If you have a little extra time on your hands, there's never been a better reason for a getaway to Paris than our special fare." The special offer sold out. Madison Avenue research indicates that ads which leave potential customers smiling have lasting positive impacts.

All business is show business

Stanley Arnold managed one of his father's many Pick-N-Pay stores in Cleveland, Ohio. One year a blizzard hit town and paralyzed the city. Employees came to work but didn't have much to do. Arnold began to think funny and came up with an great promotional idea. He had his employees make snowballs — about 8,000 of them. Then he had the snowballs placed into grapefruit cartons and taken to a deep-freeze facility.

Next, Arnold went to the Weather Bureau to find out when the hottest day of the year would be. With this information, he went to New York and met with the president of General Foods. They put together a promotional campaign for a sale scheduled to take place in mid-July — the projected hottest day of the year. Summer came and on the big day the temperature was 100 degrees. The sale was called "A Blizzard of Values" and featured 40,000 samples of General Foods' products. These were given away along with nearly 8,000 grapefruit-sized snowballs — on the hottest day of the year! Police had to be called to control the crowds during this five-day frenzy. Thousands of customers were introduced to new products and publicity flourished for both the store and General Foods. There's no business like show business!

Talking about food, who hasn't tasted Spam at one time or another in their life — probably in an army mess hall, a school cafeteria or at summer camp. It has been the butt of numerous jokes. But Hormel Foods demonstrated their sense of humor while, at the same time, promoting their product. A couple of years ago, building on some self-directed humor, they introduced a line of merchandise with the Spam logo. These included earrings, water bottles, T-shirts, underwear and other items of clothing.

During the Golden Globe Awards, actress Christine Lahti was caught in the bathroom when her name was called. So, as Hollywood readied itself for the Oscars, the makers of Kaopectate realized an opportunity. They sent all twenty acting nominees "Kaopectate Oscar Relief Baskets" with a letter stating it hoped the baskets would give the nervous nominees a "solid performance" throughout the evening. The news media got wind of the story and the resultant publicity made Kaopectate a winner at the Oscars.

For the average person or firm, television is the quickest way to get live widespread coverage nowadays. But in the medium of television, soundbites are the ticket. How can we hope to make the case for ourselves or our businesses when our statements are dissected into parcels of information only six to eight seconds long? The best way is to make your gem novel and humorous. This is the closest you can come to ensuring its use.

Contests

Contests are a great way to get publicity and promote your product or service. A garage door company sponsors an "ugly door contest." The prize is — what else — a new garage door. A San Diego bar holds an annual "Elvis Lives!" evening every January 8 to celebrate the King's birthday. It includes an Elvis and Pricilla look-alike contest. On Valentine's Day, a local pet supply store sponsors a Singles Pet Mixer for pets and their people.

> "Join our annual charity Mardi Gras 10K Run & Walk.
> The second most fun you'll ever have panting."

When the Chicago White Sox found their attendance down some thirty-five percent they conjured up a series of "wacky weeknight" themes. Among them is Dog Day of Summer, in which Rover gets in free. The evening featured a pre-game costume parade that showcased canines dressed as baseball players. Old episodes of "Rin Tin Tin" played on the scoreboard and "dog acts" were provided at the gates. Another evening was called "Romance Night" and featured a nine-inning kissing contest and a special boy-girl "stag section."

The fun factor at work

Any business, service or product is appropriate for a humorous promotional approach if it's done with taste. My chiropractor had a special door mat made up after my suggestion. It reads: "Welcome, We're glad to see your back!" A doctor might have a sign in his or her waiting room that reads, "Amnesia patients must pay in advance."

A dentist might have one that says, "You don't have to floss *all* your teeth, just those you want to keep." This not only suggests that the dentist has a sense of humor and doesn't take himself too seriously, but also conveys an important message in a very effective way. One way of coming up with ideas for novel and humorous promotional opportunities is to get the book on special days, weeks and months, and then to tie in some promotion with that theme. A florist, for example, uses Good Neighbor Day to give away 1,000 roses. Recipients are given a dozen each with the stipulation that they are to keep one and give away the other eleven to different people as a way of getting acquainted or renewing a friendship.

On Interstate Route 40, somewhere near The Middle of Nowhere, Arizona, you'll find Seligman, a small burg that will make you wonder how anyone could wind up there and, if they did, why they didn't leave. But you'll notice a Herculean hamburger towering over a restaurant named Delgadillo Snow Cap. It is accompanied by giant twirling ice cream cones and a series of signs proffering malts, shakes, tacos, burritos, a dead chicken and, below all this, a white sedan convertible, draped in garland, complete with an inflatable Santa on the hood and an aluminum Christmas tree in the back seat.

The sign on the window reads, "Sorry, We Are Open," and another suggests, "If we are closed, just shove your money under the door." If you order a "small coke," you'll get a paper vessel the size of a thimble filled with about an eye-dropper's worth of syrup in fizzy soda. Juan Delgadillo, the owner, came up with this motif after he almost had an ulcer trying to cater to people. Does it work? He displays a plaque given to him by a customer. The inscription reads, "To Juan Delgadillo, king of smiles, who can laugh and make us laugh. God bless you. We all love you."

"Going out of business sale!
(We reserve the right to stay in business
if our sale is successful)"

Just north of San Diego you'll find a little Mexican restaurant with the unusual name of "Taco Auctioneers." If you'd like to eat there, plan a short wait because you will normally find a line of people at the door. The food is good and the prices are reasonable. But the real attraction is the fun atmosphere. Waiters play jokes on the customers by wearing fake Rambo chests, funny masks and crazy hats. Order a chicken burrito or a fish taco and you may find yourself looking at a large rubber chicken or a plastic trout served between a fake tortilla. They will pretend to spill coffee on you or squirt fake plastic mustard or catsup on you. Frivolity abounds and results in profits.

A movie and book from geeks

Minneapolis is home to a company founded in 1994 called The Geek Squad. If it sounds like the name of a television crime series you're not far off. The owner, Robert Stephens, is a *Dragnet* fan as well as a shrewd businessman. The office is called "Geek Squad Headquarters." Employees, who are on call twenty-four hours a day, seven days a week, dress in black slacks, starched white shirts, narrow black clip-on ties with white socks and black shoes and are known as "special agents." They drive cars with Geek Squad logos on the side and flash official badges. The company is in the unlikely business of computer support services and is described by Stephens as "a military psychosis of comic proportion." He says the humor not only makes the job fun for employees, but relieves stress for the customer. A book detailing the squad's secret tips is scheduled for release by Simon and Schuster and a fictional movie based on the real Geek Squad, to be produced by Disney, is in the works.

Customers who show up at Chicago's Planet Cafe in their jammies get a ten percent discount. Ever since the Planet adopted its come-as-you-are breakfast rules, diners have been arriving in shorts, pajama bottoms, big fuzzy slippers and see-through negligees. Not only does this policy attract customers who have a penchant for the unusual but it also pulls in those who want to be a part of the fun atmosphere.

Responding to restaurants offering free meals if you're not served within a specified period of time, a local soda fountain has a notice on its menu that advises: "If you're not served in five minutes, you'll get served in eight or nine, maybe twelve minutes. Just relax." Another such disclaimer reportedly appears on Haventree Software's EasyFlow program. It reads, "If EasyFlow doesn't work: tough. If you lose millions because EasyFlow messes up, it's you who is out the millions, not us. If you don't like this disclaimer: tough. We reserve the right to do the absolute minimum provided by law, up to and including nothing. This is basically the same disclaimer that comes with all software packages, but ours is written in plain English and theirs is legalese. We didn't want to include any disclaimer at all, but our lawyers insisted."

These kinds of quips create feel-good smiles which ingratiate businesses with their customers. A Small Business Administration executive shared a story of creative marketing with a humorous flair. The Small Business Administration, he said, arranged a loan to a Florida company proposing to combine a veterinary hospital with a taxidermy studio. The company motto was particularly creative: "One Way or Another, You Get Your Dog Back."

Offbeat humor

The more conventional the product or service, the more need for some unusual humorous theatrics to promote it. But even offbeat businesses scratch around for witty ideas to help them along. Vidal Herrera, a longtime investigator for the Los Angeles County Coroner's Office came up with the idea of a chain of nationwide franchises that offer autopsy services. He is a shameless promoter who has vanity plates on his car (YSPOTA, which spells autopsy in a rearview mirror) and has a 1-800-AUTOPSY phone number painted on his vans. He is reportedly planning to sponsor a team in the next L.A. Marathon called the "Stiffs."

As in the above case, such shenanigans can be controversial. When the Canadian Football League was looking for attention, it came up with the marketing slogan "Our Balls Are Bigger." While it isn't even true (their balls used to be bigger than the NFL but are now the same size) it brought them the attention — albeit some negative — that they wanted.

Dan Quayle — who once misspelled "potato" at a school spelling bee while he was vice president — was enlisted to do an advertising spot for Wavy Lay's Potato Chips.

Sometimes the very name of your business can generate attention. Puns are probably most used in this regard. In Evanston, Illinois, folks can visit a hot-dog joint called Mustard's Last Stand. Bostonians can have their catering done by Currier and Chives and Chicago residents who need a septic tank cleaner can call on the Wizard of Ooze. Hair salons call themselves such names as From Hair to Eternity, United Hairlines and The Best Little Hairhouse. When a pet store on Chicago's North Side came up with the name of Let's Pet, a fancy new pet boutique opened nearby calling itself Groomingdales.

Business slogans are also a fertile area for humor. Take Slimm's Sanitation in Greeley, Colorado, where the proud motto is, "We're number one in the number two business," or Ball Septic Service in Durango, Colorado, that admits, "My Business Stinks." Also in Durango is the Durango Muffler Service that confesses, "Our business is exhausting." In Pullman, Washington, you'll find Art's Electric that advertises, "Let us remove your shorts." And in Hollister, California, the Hey Diddle Diaper Service asks would-be customers to "Let us lighten your load."

Advertising

William G. Shaw was a stand-up comic at age twenty-two but decided he couldn't support his wife and infant child on his earnings. So he became president of Pilot Pen Corp. of America and used skills borrowed from his former career to take it from $1 million to $83 million a year in sales. He uses his ability to think funny to dream up ads that boost Pilot's sales. One featured a woman asking her psychiatrist, "Is it sick to love a pen?" The answer: "Not if it's a Pilot pen." Sales doubled the year after the ad was released. Then, after seeing sales almost triple in 1977, he reworked the ad into another successful campaign — "If it's sick to love a pen, then the whole world must be crazy." True, it isn't hilarious, but it has a humorous spin and that's enough to set the mood and do the trick.

Probably the most highly visible use of humor for business purposes is in advertising. Year after year, the humorous touch resonates with consumers. In 1996 the most effective ad campaign in the USA was for Energizer batteries — featuring the bunny that, like the ads, just kept going and going and going. You probably have your own favorite ad or commercial. And you may have noticed that, whether it is Jerry Seinfeld for American Express, the Maytag repairman, or a famous athlete; the products are pitched with a laugh and a smile. A little reflection makes the point — humor sells!

Speaking of funny ads with athletes, who can forget Bob Ueker, the former baseball player way up there in the stadium cheap seats? Who can forget the football players dismissing water polo because the horses couldn't run in the water? And you must have noticed that Snoopy is working for Metropolitan Life Insurance Company and the Little Tramp of silent movie fame is already a veteran salesman for IBM. A whole book could be written on this one subject and the approaches are as diverse as there are ideas.

Little Caesar's Pizza has a reputation for superb humorous ads. In fact, the commercials were so popular that the campaign became a victim of its own success. The special brand of offbeat humor that permeated their ads brought actual belly laughs. When they created the next series, although funny, they didn't go over as well and were considered less than successful — even though they were funnier than most other commercials.

For decades it was thought that humor had no place in financial advertising. But in 1981, the chairman of Phoenix-based Arizona Banc-West Corp., Don Tostenrud, decided he wanted a fresh approach for his $2 billion-asset company and its main subsidiary, Arizona Bank. What he got from his ad agency, Benton & Bowles, was a series of skits featuring Bob and Ray, then a popular comedy team. In the sequence of commercials, Bob and Ray appeared trying to open the Bank of Bob and Ray and compete with "the smartest bank" — the Arizona Bank. In one such spot they were roaming the desert with their "Wandering Teller machine" — their answer to Arizona Bank's statewide 24-hour cash machines. In another, they were trying to steal business from the Arizona Bank by parading before their competitor in a sandwich sign reading "The Bank of Bob and Ray: We Have Dough to Blow." The results of the $3.5 million campaign: 97 percent of all Arizona consumers recognized the bank and their new-account growth rate increased 150 percent.

Telegraphing benefits

Humorous ads not only entertain, they imbed a positive image in the minds of consumers. One such memorable ad that knocked my socks off was one for Hanes featuring a man's feet wearing socks riddled with holes. The banner read, "Buy Cheap Socks And You'll Pay Through The Toes," but the copy focused on their durability stating that Hanes socks are made to last longer. The ad was replete with puns such as, "socks that are made to last long after others are on their last legs," so it will be "longer before you're footing the bill for a new pair." This is effective humor telegraphing benefits instantly and clearly.

My favorite ad with a humorous theme is from London where an enterprising ad agency figured out how to profit from the President Clinton-Monica Lewinsky scandal. As you may recall, the flap included ubiquitous showings of some video footage wherein the president encounters Lewinsky at a political rally and gives her a hug. The agency developed an advertisement for a computer program that allows users to remove undesired items from photographs. An ad in the *Daily Telegraph* showed the now infamous image of the hug with a caption proclaiming, "the Olympus Digital lets you crop out anything that ruins your image." Lewinsky had disappeared from the photo. It not only got plenty of attention in England but earned mention in *Newsweek* magazine.

Sometimes products enjoy a positive PR jolt serendipitously. Kimberly-Clark Corp. got an estimated $350,000 worth of free advertising when professional football coach Bill Parcells of the New York Jets made a complimentary postgame remark about his rookie kicker. Said Parcells, "We're trying to get this kid off diapers and into his street clothes. Today, we took those Huggies off."

As these examples demonstrate, humor is a great way to draw attention to and promote a product or service. If your message doesn't get noticed, it can't possibly communicate. Punctuating your promotional themes with humor also makes them memorable. Remember, smiles create warm feelings which subliminally transfer to your product or service. Here's an ad for a hair salon: "Someday we will live in a world free of shallow people who make judgments based on physical appearance. Until then, make your color and perm appointment at the Jon Giannoa Salon."

Even government can appreciate the value of humor in advertising. As part of its campaign to encourage drivers to use public transportation, New York City Transit posted this sign on its buses: "Ride the bus. Leave the swearing to us."

Vanderbilt University found itself the doormat of its football league, having had only three winning seasons in thirty-six years. After the Commodores went two and nine in 1996, the university began using humor in an effort to sell more season tickets. They ran a series of five fifteen-second commercials featuring the new football coach, Woody Widenhofer, and several of his top players in humorous skits. In one, a senior linebacker takes a bite out of the coach's hat. In another, Widenhofer calls a hulking lineman "Tiny." The ad campaign was built on the tag line, "Have fun. Expect to win."

Promotion should be consistent with your image

Humor can also be used to counter the efforts of a competitor or other business antagonist. An owner of ten office furniture warehouse stores in Chicago became annoyed when he saw a bank's offer of free calculators to its new customers. So he countered by offering the bank's product (free *money*) to *his* new clientele. This must have worked because he followed it with a promotion involving his version of a sidewalk sale — he broke up the sidewalk outside one of his stores and gave autographed pieces to customers.

The Plough and the Stars Irish restaurant in Philadelphia holds a Banshee Wailing Contest. (A banshee is a ghostly female spirit of Irish folklore, recognizable by her haunting moans and wails.) The winner gets a free dinner and reigns for a full year as the restaurant's official moaner.

Eddie Murphy sends out Christmas cards containing microchips that, when pressed, laugh just like him. Steve Martin, when asked for his autograph, hands out a card that says: "This certifies that you have had a personal encounter with me and that you found me warm, polite, intelligent and funny."

Of course, one way people try to promote themselves is by use of the unusual business card. This is an area where you can use some humorous dramatics to enhance your image and promote yourself.

A San Diego attorney who specializes in paternity and child-support cases has these messages on the backs of his business cards: "SURGEON GENERAL'S WARNING: Clinical Studies Have Proved That Sexual Intercourse May Cause Babies. ATTORNEY GENERAL'S WARNING: Willful Failure to Support One's Minor Child in California is a Misdemeanor Punishable by Both Fine and Imprisonment."

Here are a few of the more innovative: A dentist who produces the Floss Card, a piece of plastic with a string of floss hanging from it. An erotica store attaches condoms to its cards.

Ken Erdman is founder of the Business Card Museum in Pennsylvania and a collector of these offbeat promotional gimmicks. He says, "a business card has achieved greatness when the person who receives it asks the question, 'Oh. May I keep this?'" His collection of creative cards includes one from an Atlantic City writer that unfolds to reveal a pop-up typewriter. When you open it, a page rolls out reading the words: "Am I the type writer you're looking for?"

Another is from a company called Todco Pest Control with the slogan "Putting the bite on pests since 1959." It is a thinly sliced wood shaving with gnaw marks at the corner. When you are trying to promote some thing or some body, put on your "thinking-funny cap" and try to come up with a humorous ploy to further your goals. That's what Jeff Vlaming of Minnesota did when he wanted to write for the popular television series *X-Files*. Besides being notoriously difficult to reach, executive producer Chris Carter didn't seem to be impressed with scripts sent to him by Vlaming and his agent. So, drawing on his skills acquired when he was with an advertising agency back in the 1980s, he devised a prop and mailed it to Carter. It was a space-alien embryo he sculpted from a sponge. He placed it in a pickle jar and covered it with a paper bag that read, "My God, Mulder, it's trying to communicate!" When the bag was removed there was this little alien with a sign that read, "Jeff Vlaming is ready to pitch ideas." The humor solution paid off. Vlaming got the job.

Critical appeal

Why do two out of every three principal ads for major products employ a humorous theme? Because it sells. Research shows that folks would rather be entertained than lectured. Humor stimulates attention and increases product appeal. The fact that most of the really effective commercials have been humorous or fun has compounded the trend and even spurred more and more regional and local businesses to peddle their products with commercials that are goofy, whimsical, silly and sometimes downright obnoxious. A case in point is Crazy Eddie, a New York area consumer-electronics chain with a pitchman who raves about "insane" prices and "Christmas sales" in July.

Instead of copying the slick ad style of Madison Avenue ad factories, local advertisers are turning out low-budget promotions that they often write and produce themselves. Their mantra is nothing is too ridiculous if it catches a viewer's attention. Crazy Eddie's commercials feature announcers attacking water beds with chain saws and dressing up like gorillas and yelling, "You'll go bananas!" In some cases, these homemade off-the-wall routines have caused a company's business to increase one hundred percent or more virtually overnight. Another example of the offbeat commercial is Cal Worthington, a Los Angeles auto dealer so well known he has been parodied on the late night shows for his wild ads. He appears wearing a cowboy hat and parades around a car lot with animals ranging from pigs and tigers to hippos and elephants, each of which he refers to as "my dog Spot." These goofy ads often deliver spectacular results.

Bozo can bring in the bucks

Gallery Furniture of Houston was struggling to survive when they launched a madcap campaign. Although lacking in broadcasting experience, owner James McIngvale ad-libbed spots in which he blabbered as fast as he could for fifty-five seconds and then, in the last five seconds, leaped into the air holding a cluster of dollar bills while shouting, "Gallery Furniture really will save! . . . You! . . . Money!" Since he first went airborne, his sales have soared one thousand percent and he says it saved the company. Acting like a bozo can bring in the bucks!

If you are considering this approach, here are some tips to keep in mind. First, ask yourself if humor is compatible with your product or service. If you can do it in good taste, the answer is almost always yes. Keep the humor relevant and related to the message and product. Know your audience and approach them considering their level of sophistication. This will determine whether they will respond to slapstick, satire, repartee or routines based on current events.

Develop your humor from recognizable situations. If they are likely to stay current on national or global events, play off of them. If not, use other, more mundane themes. Don't use jokes. Develop comical situations and characters your audience can identify. Start with your product or service and expand it into a simple storyline studded with comical dialogue or monologue.

Don't be afraid to be really zany. Exaggeration is one of the most effective forms of humor. So go for it, but stop short of overkill and keep it wholesome and in good taste. National Airlines had an ad you might remember that was centered on the phrase "Fly Me." It was a double entendre that proved offensive to women's feminist sensibilities. Don't let the comedy obscure the message; it should carry it, rather than conceal or upstage it.

Keep in mind that the object is to heighten attention and interest and make it stand out from your competition. Be sure it appeals to the head, heart and funny bone.

Selling with humor

Some years ago, television host Johnny Carson had a guest who billed himself as "The World's Greatest Salesman." I'll always remember their exchange. Johnny asked him to "sell me something." The guest asked Johnny what he wanted him to sell. Johnny picked up an ashtray from his desk and said, "Sell me this." The exchange that followed went something like this:

Salesman: "Why would you want to buy this? (holding ashtray)
Johnny: "Well, I could put my cigarette ashes in it."
Salesman: "Why else would you want it?"
Johnny: "Well, besides being functional, it looks good. It's decorative."
Salesman: "How much would you pay for it?"
Johnny: "Oh, I don't know. Maybe $5, maybe $10."
Salesman: "Sold!"

It was a masterful job and a great lesson in salesmanship. He had Johnny's attention and interest. It was a matter of defining benefits and demonstrating that they outweighed costs. The process of selling is often described with the acronym AIDA: Attention, Interest, Desire, Action. But they must happen in that order. If you can't get their attention you simply can't communicate *anything* to them — much less attract their interest. It is the most important part of the sales process because if you don't get an audience, you've lost the transaction. Humor can be the key to step one. Humor gets attention.

Creativity — the cornerstone of selling

There are many, many examples of cases where simply getting the appointment meant success. Nothing happens until you get your prospect's ear. In 47 B.C. Cleopatra had herself rolled up in a carpet and smuggled into Caesar's office. He admired her chutzpah and bought her idea for an alliance. *There's always a way to get in the door* and creativity is the key!

When I sold insurance in Ohio there was a man by the name of Ben Feldman who was (and remains) a legend in the business of selling life insurance. One of his secrets was getting in to see people who were generally inaccessible to his competitors. But Ben would go to the executive's secretary, hand her a $100 bill and his business card. He'd say, "I know Mr. Bigalow is very busy and that his time is worth a great deal. Please give him this $100 and tell him that I'd like to buy five minutes of his time. The approach was so unique and practical that he usually got in to see the person. Once there he would use his other sales skills to interest and sell his prospect.

I recall an investment salesman who had a business card with the number 12,639 in the upper left corner. Recipients would invariably ask about the number. He would respond that 12,639 was the number of meals they'll buy after the age of sixty-five if they lived to normal life expectancy. "If you pay just two dollars per meal," he would explain, "you'll need at least $50,556 for you and your spouse." Then he would add, "Would you care to spend a few minutes discussing retirement investments?" Nothing in either of these two examples is funny but they demonstrate the efficacy of using theatrics to gain an audience. When you can punctuate it with humor, the approach becomes doubly effective.

Breaking through the barriers

Again, we see how getting the attention of your prospective buyer is critical to the selling process. A primary rule of selling is you must sell yourself before you sell your product. If people are laughing with you, it's pretty hard for them not to like you. And if they like you, they're more open to your ideas and propositions. Humor will increase your "likability factor."

Recently, I read about a salesman who was having difficulty getting in to see his prospect. As he walked through the airport for his flight home, he noticed a flight insurance machine. He bought a half-million dollar policy and named the prospect as his beneficiary. Then he mailed it to him with a note saying, "My last thoughts were of you!" On his next trip to the area, he called on the fellow and sold him.

Another salesperson, frustrated after failing to get an appointment with her potential client, had a homing pigeon delivered to the prospect by a Western Union messenger. Tied to the pigeon's leg was a tag which read: "If you'd like more information about our product, just throw our representative out the window." An appointment and sale followed.

When I told one audience about these humorous methods, a lady shared her own similar technique with me. She would buy up old baby dolls at garage sales. Then when she was unable to get in to see a prospect, she would send in an arm from the doll with a note stating, "I'd give my right arm to talk to you!" She told me this worked wonders for her. Another individual bought the remaining stock of a failing doll company. He dismembered them and kept the hands and feet. He approaches prospective clients by sending them a package of doll parts and a note that reads, "I'd like to get a foot in the door and give you a hand." If you sell a service or product, look for innovative ways to circumvent the resistance you are encountering.

Thinking funny can pay other dividends too! I read about a secretary who brought a salesman's card to her boss, who tore it in half and threw it in the wastepaper basket. He snapped, "Tell him I'm too busy to see him." When she delivered the message, the salesman, obviously thinking he had nothing to lose, said, "Okay, but ask him if I can have my card back. They're expensive." In a few minutes, the secretary returned from her boss's office and handed the

salesman a quarter. The salesman handed her another card and said, "Tell him they're two for a quarter." He got to see his prospect!

There are many variations of this. You can send a cake with a message on it. The point is, humor is the best tool to get into a selling situation. Do it differently with innovation — and humor if possible.

When all-pro football player, Reggie White, was trying to decide on which team he wanted to play, a newspaper reporter asked him how he would choose his new home. White, an ordained minister, replied, "God will tell me where to go." He subsequently got a phone call from Green Bay Packers coach Mike Holmgren, who left a message on his answering machine saying, "This is God. I want you to go to Green Bay." Reggie, who did decide on the Wisconsin team, must have appreciated Holmgren's sense of humor. When he arrived, he was told by quarterback Bret Favre that there were three reasons he welcomed him there. One, it was a great football town; two, he could make a difference there, and three, Favre didn't want to be hit by him any more.

Getting to the prospect with humor

A fellow professional speaker relates an experience he had in getting an engagement. He called his prospect, a television industry association executive, numerous times without a response. When he finally reached her, she said, impatiently, "My desk is piled high with brochures from speakers who want to talk at my convention. Just send yours and I'll review it."

Joe pictured a desk overflowing with mountains of brochures and knew he had to find a way to make his stand out. He bought a ceramic piggybank the size of a basketball. Then he stuffed his brochure through the money slot and sent the pig with a hammer and note that read, "Inside is the secret to helping your members make more money in advertising sales. Break me!" He called a few days later and was told they had found the pig so cute they used a coat hanger to fish the brochure out. Not surprisingly he got the job!

I read about a fellow who uses a hand-puppet of a monkey to gain entrance to his prospects' offices. To get his foot in the door he charms receptionists into announcing to their bosses, "There's a man out here with a monkey who would like to see you!" Invariably, the person in charge comes out to at least have a look, sometimes bringing others along. Prospects get caught up in the act and the salesman uses the puppet to explain his products — specialty items for promotions and gifts.

If you sell — and we all do, even if it's just our ideas — look for ways to use a similar technique to pitch or promote your product or service. A woman tells about her husband who practices his golf swing on their lawn, usually breaking a window or two. One year, she relates, the number of broken windows rose to four. The following Spring a parcel arrived, addressed to her husband. It was a box of golf balls. The enclosed note read, "Have a good season. From Mike, your window man." Here a little humor is used to build a reservoir of good will.

Another example of creative humor in persuasion is from the Minneapolis Red Cross soliciting blood donations. They posted this notice: "Before Going on Vacation, Donate Blood. Mosquitoes Don't Give Coffee & Donuts — We Do!" A couple facing retirement was scouting around for a nice place to live out their golden years. In the town of Summerland in Santa Barbara County, California, they saw a signpost that read:

SUMMERLAND
Population 3001
Feet above sea level 208
Established 1870
Total 5079

They decided to settle there because they appreciated the town's sense of humor.

Selling yourself

A candidate who applied for acceptance to New York University received the following request: "In order for the admissions staff of our college to get to know you, the applicant, better, we ask that you answer the following question: Are there any significant experiences you have had, or accomplishments you have realized, that have helped to define you as a person?"

He responded accordingly: "I am a dynamic figure, often seen scaling walls and crushing ice. I have been known to remodel train stations on my lunch breaks, making them more efficient in the area of heat retention. I translate ethnic slurs for Cuban refugees, I write award-winning operas, I manage time efficiently.

Occasionally, I tread water for three days in a row.

I woo women with my sensuous and godlike trombone playing. I can pilot bicycles up severe inclines with unflagging speed and I cook thirty-minute brownies in twenty minutes. I am an expert in stucco, a veteran in love and an outlaw in Peru. Using only a hoe and a large glass of water, I once single-handily defended a small village in the Amazon basin from a horde of ferocious army ants. I play bluegrass cello, I was scouted by the Mets, I am the subject of numerous documentaries. When I'm bored, I build large suspension bridges in my yard. I enjoy urban hang gliding. On Wednesdays, after school, I repair electrical appliances free of charge.

I am an abstract artist, a concrete analyst, and a ruthless bookie. Critics worldwide swoon over my original line of corduroy evening wear. I don't perspire. I am a private citizen, yet I receive fan mail. I have been caller number nine and have won the weekend passes. Last Summer I toured New Jersey with a traveling centrifugal-force demonstration. I bat .400. My deft floral arrangements have earned me fame in international botany circles. Children trust me.

I can hurl tennis rackets at small moving objects with deadly accuracy. I once read *Paradise Lost, Moby Dick* and *David Copperfield* in one day and still had time to refurbish an entire dining room that evening. I know the exact location of every item in the supermarket. I have performed several covert operations with the CIA. I sleep once a week; when I do sleep, I sleep in a chair. While on vacation in Canada I successfully negotiated with a group of terrorists who had seized a small bakery. The laws of physics do not apply to me. I balance, I weave, I dodge, I frolic, and my bills are all paid. On weekends, to let off steam, I participate in full-contact origami. Years ago I discovered the meaning of life but forgot to write it down. I have made extraordinary four course meals using only a mouli and a toaster oven.

I breed prizewinning clams. I have won bullfights in San Juan, Cliff diving competitions in Sri Lanka, and spelling bees at the Kremlin. I have played Hamlet, I have performed open-heart surgery, and I have spoken with Elvis.

But I have not yet gone to college."

The applicant was accepted. Whether you are applying to a school, interviewing for a job, or attempting to make a new friend or stimulate romance; humor will ensure your positive reception in a manner that cannot be matched. In selling either your ideas, service or product, don't forget to draw on a little showmanship, including humor.

Chapter Four

Make Your Point in Only 10 Seconds

"Laughter is the shortest distance between two people."
—Victor Borge

Football coaches are driven nuts when their players celebrate ostentatiously in the end zone following a touchdown. In spite of lectures, fines and other forms of persuasion it continues. Lou Holtz, when he was coach of Notre Dame, seemed to solve the problem by telling his players, "When you get to the end zone, act like you've been there before!"

It's almost impossible to overstate the importance of good communication skills. What you say and how you say it will determine how people evaluate you. Good speaking is the key to leadership and has been responsible for the rise and fall of world leaders and factory workers. Whatever your occupation, the ability to persuade can raise your career to new heights. As you become more successful, the probability that you'll be speaking before groups increases. You'll have occasion to address employees, customers, board members, bankers, political bodies as well as clubs and groups to which you belong. When you're speaking, whether it is for business or personal reasons, chances are your objective is to persuade.

Whether you're communicating one-on-one, speaking to a group, engaging in a debate or writing a letter, report or whatever, using humor is probably the best method of making your point in the quickest and most effective way. Humor closes the emotional distance between people and builds a sympathetic bridge. One important rule of communication is that, long after the message has been forgotten, your image and the feelings generated by it will live on in the memory of your audience. Another rule is that any message is useless unless people hear and remember it.

> *"A sense of humor is the ability to perceive and isolate the humorous element in ordinary conversation."*
>
> —Anon.

If you need to be convinced about the importance of likability in persuasion, watch some of the television shows that feature debates, such as *Firing Line*, *Crossfire* or the *News Hour with Jim Lehrer*. Observe the participants and make your own assessment of the effect of likability on persuasion. You'll see ample demonstrations of the use of humor to bypass conscious resistance.

When the MGM opened in Las Vegas, they found themselves with numerous employees of various ethnic backgrounds, cultures and languages. How would they explain their fringe benefit package so that it could be understood and appreciated? They came up with a Groucho look-alike and made a film explaining the various benefits. Instead of receiving a lecture, the employees were entertained. Just the idea that a person has the potential to be entertaining is usually enough to grab attention and heighten interest. Let's review the different communicative situations in which you are likely to be engaged and see how humor can facilitate your message and help make your point in literally seconds.

One-on-one

Most friendships are built on laughter. When you communicate with smiles and laughter, a bond is established and you can make your point. Longtime friends normally laugh a great deal together. That's why they've stayed friends. Humor, fun and laughter serve to cement the relationship. Being able to joke with each other means you're comfortable together. It denotes an unguarded openness. Remember, tension and trust have an inverse relationship. When one is up, the other is down.

If you are trying to change someone's opinion in a one-on-one situation, keep in mind that it's not done instantaneously — no matter how correct your position is or how well you articulate it. People don't usually throw up their hands and say, "Of course! You're right and I'm wrong about that." You change minds by planting seeds and allowing them to germinate in a healthy, non-threatening environment. Humor is an excellent vehicle for transmitting such seeds. It works best when the humor is directed at the situation or, better yet, self-directed. It will seldom work if you've made fun of the other person. This conveys the notion that, if they accept your position, they buy into a package that includes their stupidity.

> *"Another thing that man can do that the lower animals can't is*
> *stand up in front of a crowd and put both feet in his mouth."*
> —Anon.

Speaking to a group

Mark Twain made his point rather cogently when he observed that when he was eighteen his father was very stupid. But, he said, when he became twenty-one he could never understand how his father had gotten so smart in those three years. Every time I see an article about someone who has a reputation for persuasiveness, I scan it for reference to humor. There was a recent article about our United Nations' representative, Bill Richardson. It covered his many achievements in international diplomacy — especially the release of hostages from North Korea, Iraq and Cuba. Sure enough, it discussed how he used humor on the poker-faced North Koreans. It quoted Richardson as saying, "When they started smiling, I knew I was getting to them." Humor connects us.

We have a saying among professional speakers: "You don't have to use humor in your talk; only if you expect to get paid for it." Humor is absolutely essential in making group presentations. The most serious message will include some humor if it is delivered by an adroit speaker. Even modern eulogies contain humor. It is used to recall the lighter moments of one's life. Most of us want to be remembered for how we lived rather than how we died. A little humor also begins the healing process.

The magic bullet

Communications guru Roger Ailes coaches CEOs of America's top corporations and includes among his clients former presidents Ronald Reagan and George Bush. Ailes says that when you get up to speak, you have just seven seconds to make that important first impression on your audience. How you approach the lectern, how you reach for the microphone and the expression on your face are all parts of the image you project before you even utter a word. But when you do open your presentation, what you say is critical as well. That is why it is a good idea to open with humor. It breaks the ice, holds attention, relaxes the audience and establishes rapport. It enhances your "likability factor," a term Ailes calls "the magic bullet."

You should not feel *obliged* to use humor to open a talk. If it makes you uncomfortable, skip it. But with some thought and practice, you should be able to use humor to send the magic bullet. A strong, warm beginning puts you in control and gets you off to a good start. If you are going to be speaking for a brief period, you could begin by saying, "as Henry VIII used to tell his wives, 'I'll only be keeping you for a short time.'" The best humorous openings are personalized to the situation or audience and are mildly self-deprecating to the speaker. This approach works best because the audience will appreciate the tailored remarks, and self-directed humor is always the best received — especially in this kind of setting.

Humor can be included in just about anything as long as you remember the rule of AT&T (appropriate, timely, tasteful). Such things as annual reports are ripe for adding some color and flair with a bit of wit. Warren Buffett, the driving force behind Berkshire Hathaway, uses humor effectively in their annual reports. Here are just a few items from some of his:

On inflation: "Like virginity, a stable price level seems capable of maintenance, but not of restoration." (1981)

"If corporate pregnancy is going to be the consequence of corporate mating, the time to face that fact is before the moment of ecstasy." (1982)

"No matter how great the talent or effort, some things just take time: you can't produce a baby in one month by getting nine women pregnant." (1985)

Buffett cited Woody Allen, who pointed out the advantage of open-mindedness by saying, "I can't understand why more people aren't bisexual because it automatically doubles your chances for a date on Saturday night."

Royal regards

When Queen Elizabeth II visited this country, she was inadvertently provided with a podium for a much taller queen. The press dubbed her address "the talking hat." The very next day, she was scheduled to speak again. Playing off the situation, she opened with, "I hope you can see me!" It's only mildly funny at best, but, because of who she is, it had the effect of endearing her to the audience and resulted in a standing ovation. In 1986 the Queen was touring the island of Tonga, a less than enthusiastic member of the Commonwealth. As she was leaving one of the events held in her honor, someone threw an egg at her as she entered her limousine. The egg spattered all over her clothes. The next morning she was scheduled to address the parliament. Everyone was aware of her

68

humiliation and she knew they were all waiting to see how she would deal with this outrage. She opened her talk by saying, "While I do enjoy an occasional egg, I much prefer receiving it with my breakfast meal." By joking about the situation she demonstrated leadership, strength, dignity, courage as well as her lack of intimidation.

If you are addressing a group, it is probably because you are perceived to have greater knowledge or experience in the subject matter than the audience. Self-directed humor is a way of ingratiating yourself with them. It removes or diminishes any imagined threat of superiority or concomitant intimidation. It closes the distance.

My former speech coach told me about the "wet soap rule." He explained that it came from famous playwright, Noel Coward. Basically, it states that when the audience is tense, you must become relaxed. Squeezing a bar of wet soap will only send it shooting out of your hand. But if you hold it gently, you maintain control. So, to the extent that you find your listeners anxious or strained, it becomes important for you to relax — the opposite of your natural tendency. Using humor relaxes both the audience and you.

After comedienne Totie Fields had her leg amputated, she appeared before an audience and used the experience as the basis for a joke. Everyone knew about the unfortunate situation, so she seized upon it to create some humor to put it aside and, at the same time, relax the audience. A similar situation occurred when Joan Rivers appeared on television following the suicide of her husband. She broke the tension by cracking that he had asked to be cremated and his ashes distributed in Neiman Marcus — where he knew she would come and visit every day.

Capitalizing on the obvious

Phyllis Diller once broke her arm and had to make an appearance wearing a sling. Gene Perrett, one of her writers, tells how she called him for some humor to play off of her situation. He came up with the following opening line: "Have any of you read *The Joy of Sex*? Well there is a misprint on page 98." She used it to acknowledge what was obvious to everyone and to dismiss it with humor.

On a recent trip to make a presentation, the airline lost one of my bags— the one with my shoes and business suits. I was forced to go on stage looking like a dork. I acknowledged my appearance and dismissed it in my opening by calling attention to it. I then told them that while I was from California, I didn't dress *this* peculiarly and explained about the lost baggage. I was uncomfortable with my appearance and the humorous remark dismissed it for me as well as the audience. These quick, self-directed humorous comments go over well and the laughter is relaxing to the speaker as well as the audience.

Here's one that will almost always get a laugh: "I'd like you to know that when I'm talking, it doesn't upset me to see people looking at their watches. However, I am bothered when I notice folks shaking them." It helps to actually shake your own watch while delivering the punch line.

Along this same line, economist John Kenneth Galbraith was noted for the lengthiness of his speeches. Galbraith tells his audiences that his wife assures him that they may not be a great deal *wiser* after his talks but they are always a great deal *older*.

> *"A warm smile is the universal language of kindness."*
> —William Arthur Ward

Here is another great way to get your speech started with some self-deprecating humor: "I was standing in another part of the building earlier going over my notes, when a woman came up to me and said, "Say aren't you _____?" I said, "Why yes!" and she said, "Aren't you the speaker for this evening?" I said, "Yes." She said, "Are you nervous?" I said, "Why no!" She said, "Then what are you doing here in the women's rest room?" (And, of course, the situation can be reversed to take place in the men's room.)

Stay away from introducing your quip with a trite phrase such as, "A funny thing happened to me on the way here" or, "I heard a good joke the other day." Also, try to tie the humorous line into either the introduction or the subsequent remark. This is a way of making it relevant.

Keep in mind that in opening an address with some humor, it doesn't have to be a joke. Humor takes other forms. Here's an opening from David Roderick, Chairman of U.S. Steel: "Thank you for all those kind words, but I'm reminded of the fellow who was once introduced at a similar gathering as the most gifted businessman in the country — as evidenced by the fact that he had made a million dollars in California oil. When he rose to speak, he appeared a bit embarrassed. The facts as reported were essentially correct, he said, but he felt compelled to state that it wasn't oil, it was coal ... and it wasn't California ... it was Pennsylvania ... and it wasn't a million ... it was a hundred thousand ... and it wasn't him ... it was his brother ... and he didn't *make* it ... he *lost* it! Matters of fact aside, though, I'm grateful for those kind words and for this opportunity to talk with you today."

Constructing the segue

We'll look at segues later in the chapter but let's look at how GM chairman Roger Smith opened his talk to the University Club of New York. "I was recently reminded of the importance of clear communication by a story — true, by the way — about a police lineup. With the robbery victim watching from behind one-way glass, each person in the lineup was asked to step forward and say, 'Give me all your money — and your watch and jewelry too — right now!' Well, the first and second guys did as they were instructed — but the third fellow stepped forward and blurted out, 'Wait a minute! *That's* not what I said!' Well I don't want any misunderstanding about what I say, so I'll try to be as clear and simple as I can." His segue was a stretch but he made it fit and, most importantly, began with his audience smiling.

One way to devise an attention-getting, witty opening is to examine yourself for any aspect you can play off of to create some humor. Everybody is from somewhere and that can always be used as the basis for an opening. Nancy Kassenbaum, the U.S. Senator from Kansas, wanted to open her first speech to the National Press Club with some humor. Using her origins, she quipped, "Toto, I have a feeling we're not in Kansas anymore." If you can't come up with an appropriate remark based on your home turf, try something about where you just came from or where you're going. Or, just work backwards and use a location and segue it into your opening.

Using the other elements of theater

I recently sat through a presentation by an excellent professional speaker. He had some visual aids on an overhead projector and used a pointer that was an arm and hand with a pointing finger rather than an ordinary arrow. The speaker, an Hispanic with brown skin, displayed his first overhead with the white arm and hand, paused, and then said, "Wait a minute, that's not right." He then supplanted the white simulated arm and hand with a brown one. It generated lots of laughter and the self-directed humor enhanced his likability factor tremendously.

It is a good idea to watch how others use humor to open their talks. With some observation and a little analysis, you'll be more comfortable using wit to break the ice with your audience.

Communicating with humor, style and flair is all part of the *theater* of persuasion. One should draw on what I like to call a communications spice cabinet. Humor is to communication what seasoning is to food. It heightens the flavor and adds new dimensions. Most food entrees require not just one, but several seasonings. Presentations also benefit from a mix of different enhancers. These spices include humor, quips, quotes, similes, definitions, anecdotes, metaphors, analogies, ad libs and other such condiments. Like a fine dish, not all will be used in every serving but a good chef will have them available.

Gee whizzers

Let's look at anecdotes and see how they can be used to give your messages more color, power and impact. I call them "gee whizzers" because that is what people should say, or at least think, upon hearing them. "Gee whizzers" are offbeat facts and other illuminating anecdotes related to the subject under discussion. Just as spices often compliment each other, so does a skillful mix of these items. Think about messages the way you thing about a delicious, flavorful dish. In addition to the salt, pepper, garlic, parsley and other spices we have already discussed, a good message might be flavored with humor, a quote from someone famous and perhaps a couple of gee whizzers.

In some cases, gee whizzers are even more illustrative than humor. Both focus attention, heighten interest and add perspective. But these gems are often better than humor in providing perspective and also leave the audience with some new information, even if it is sometimes trivial. In any case, they are generically related to humor in that they also contain the "ah ha factor."

Of course, gee whizzers can be humorous as well, packing a double punch. I just received a newly published book in the mail from an author who is a friend and speaking colleague. Its title: *Thriving On Change: The Art of Using Change to Your Advantage* by Dr. Nate Booth. Here is how he opens his book: "In the 1800s, the British army faced a change. For the first time, they were confronted with a crude, yet effective, machine gun. At that time, British battle strategy was to have their soldiers — dressed in brightly colored uniforms — attack the enemy by walking toward them in long, straight rows.

"As you might imagine, that kind of strategy made it easy for the enemy's machine gun to mow down the British troops. In their initial confrontation with the machine gun, five hundred British soldiers were killed or seriously injured in a matter of minutes! When the British field commander saw the devastation, he sent the following communication back to headquarters: 'Send me five hundred more men!'"

You can see how the author very cleverly captures the readers' attention by using an opening anecdote that is a humorous gee whizzer and serves to make his point about the different ways one can deal with change.

But gee whizzers not only focus attention and heighten interest. They can be very illuminating. Imagine, for example, that you are delivering a talk on problems related to cigarette smoking. You would most certainly want to include the fact that tobacco kills 400,000 Americans every year and costs $52 billion annually in healthcare. Those are startling facts, but they lack perspective and, standing by themselves, are incomprehensible statistics with little meaning. Certain numbers need illumination to have significance. So how can gee whizzers add perspective? Let's take the two figures separately. "400,000 people! That's the equivalent of a packed jumbo jetliner crashing every 12 hours!" Or: "Smoking kills more than six times as many Americans every year as died in the entire Vietnam War!" Now the figure begins to take on meaning! Using a gee whizzer makes the figure come alive!

Incomprehensible figures

$52 billion is an almost incomprehensible figure. First of all, few people can make a mental distinction between a billion and a million. So we help them with a gee whizzer: "A million seconds equals twelve days. Can you guess how long a billion seconds is?" The answer — thirty-two years!

Here are a couple of alternative gee whizzers that also make your point: "Do you have any idea just how much a billion dollars is? If you made a stack of $1,000 bills, just one billion dollars would reach twenty-nine feet higher than the Washington Monument!" Or: "If you had a million dollars and spent $1,000 a day, you wouldn't run out of money for three years. If you had a *billion* dollars and spent $1,000 a day you wouldn't run out of money for *3,000* years."

Now, adding some humor to your gee whizzer, you can top it off with a humorous quote. Everett Dirksen, former U.S. Senator for Illinois, used to say, "A billion dollars here and a billion dollars there, and pretty soon it starts to add up to some *real* money!"

Lee Gomes, writing for The Wall Street Journal (as reported in *Reader's Digest*) explained that Bill Gates' net worth of roughly $37 billion is one of those numbers that defy easy comprehension, much like the age of the universe. He used a gee whizzer to put Mr. Gates' stratospheric wealth in down-to-earth terms. He pointed out that spending $250,000 for a Lamborghini would cost Mr. Gates — in terms of percentage of his wealth — what a 63-cent purchase would set back the average American. Then he added a second gee whizzer example: Because of the value of his time at the office, were Gates to see a $100 bill lying on the sidewalk on his way to work, he would actually lose money spending the few seconds required to stop and pick it up.

A million billion statistics

How are gee whizzers used in business? In its 1997 annual report Coca-Cola tells us that Americans drink an average of 363 Cokes a year — almost one a day. But it's only five a year in China, nine in Indonesia and thirteen in Russia. Then, Roberto Goizueta, Coke's chairman, gives us a gee whizzer by sharing some trivia. "A billion hours ago, human life appeared on Earth. A billion minutes ago, Christianity emerged. A billion seconds ago, the Beatles changed music forever. A billion Coca Colas ago was yesterday morning." Can you see how he uses a gee whizzer to illuminate the statistic and make his point in an interesting manner? A pleasant departure from the usual drab and dreary statistic-laced business report.

I was reading an article about the results of mergers. It began with an anecdote about onetime Chicago Bears fullback Bronko Nagurski. He was roughhousing with a teammate when he fell out of a second story hotel window. A crowd surrounded the dazed but unhurt athlete as he lay on the sidewalk. A policeman rushed up and asked what happened. Responded Bronko, "I don't know. I just got here myself." The article went on to state that many merged companies are in the same position. The rough and tumble of doing the deal is over, but they won't know where they stand until the dust settles. The story gets the reader's attention and heightens interest in the thrust of the article. It acts like the opening act of a main attraction in show business.

These gems can be very convincing as well. Physicist Robert Parks, an expert on space, was arguing against the space program. His argument: the cost of launching is not justified by the results. With so much enthusiasm for the space program, he needed to illustrate his contention. He reverted to a gee whizzer for effect. Pointing out that it costs $500 million per lift off, he explained that if you took lead into space and it came back gold, it would not pay for itself. Quite an incisive argument.

Historical facts

Historical facts also make good gee whizzers to illustrate or illuminate your point, focus attention and add some style, color and flair to your message. Esoteric items not only enhance your point with new information that is easy to remember but leaves the reader with the satisfaction of having learned something. A good resource for these items is the book *Famous First Facts*. It can be found in your local library. Also useful are old books containing Ripley's *Believe It or Not* items and books on the origin of words, phrases, things and customs. Incidentally, Ripley owned a vast collection of the world's most expensive automobiles — yet he never learned to drive. He was a radio pioneer but was afraid to use the telephone for fear of being electrocuted. He also drew his pictures upside-down. Some gee whizzers for your collection!

Want to illustrate the smallness of an atom? It's almost impossible to do that without an illustration. It's simply incomprehensible. So you can demonstrate how tiny it is with the following gee whizzer: If each member of the earth's entire population of five billion people joined together to count the atoms in a drop of water; each person counting one atom every second, the chore would still take more than 30,000 years.

Gee whizzers in the news

Gee whizzers can also be tied to items culled from the news. To illustrate, I just cut out two humorous items from the newspaper which I feel I can use someday. One involves the death of a monkey who almost became the mayor of Rio de Janeiro in 1988. The monkey, Tiao, was a favorite with visitors to the Rio Zoo and was launched as a candidate by the Brazilian Banana Party to attract the protest vote. The chimp racked up more than 400,000 votes to come in third. How can I use this? I can slip it into any discussion of elections, democracy, protest, animal accomplishments or South America using that aspect of my presentation for the segue.

I just clipped another item from Reuters about a 47-year-old lawyer named Andre-Francois Raffray from Arles, France who thought he had made the deal of a lifetime. In 1965, he signed a contract with Jeanne Calment, then 90, giving her $500 a month for life on the condition that she leave him her house when she died. On Christmas of 1995, Raffray died at age 77, shortly after Calment became the world's oldest known living person. She turned 121. He had paid her over $180,000 in the deal; the house is worth about $60,000. This can be tied into subjects covering longevity, bad (and good) deals, expectations, death, contracts and on and on.

If a gee whizzer is funny, that's a bonus, but they are effective regardless. The electric light bulb got its present shape because Thomas Edison accidentally dropped a screwdriver on an early light, knocking it out of its original shape and causing it to burn more brightly with increased power. This bit of esoteria can be used to illustrate how accidental occurrences influence history. I was reading the other day that a change in the average temperature of only two degrees Fahrenheit caused four hundred frigid years during the Middle Ages, and only a nine-degree change separates us from the last great ice age. I cut this out for inclusion in my files to explain by example how small changes have big effects.

Tying in a joke

During my years in urban revitalization I sat through numerous meetings of city councils. Land use is an issue that consumes much of every council meeting in every city. I recall a meeting in San Diego where a real estate development was under consideration and people were coming forward to express their support or opposition. One woman came forward to oppose the proposal and began by telling the story of a woman who had been married three times but was still a virgin. She explained that the bride was first married to a gay man, then an impotent man, and finally a real estate developer who just sat at the end of the bed telling her how wonderful it was going to be! She segued that into her point discrediting the wonderful claims being made by the proponents of the project. The entire city council broke up. She had punctuated her point with humor.

I assist executives in preparing and delivering speeches — especially adding relevant humor. Recently one of my clients (a mutual fund CEO) called to say he was to be speaking on the stock market and wanted a joke he could tie into the inevitability of its trends and the fact that no one can do anything about them. We settled on this joke to express that notion: A fellow was being interviewed for a job and was asked what he would do if he were the switchman for a railroad and he discovered two trains headed toward each other — one traveling sixty miles per hour from the East and the other going a hundred from the West. The guy says, "I'd go get my brother Clyde." The puzzled interviewer asks why he would go get his brother. He says, "Cause he ain't never seen no train wreck!"

Humorous analogies and metaphors

Who can recall the 1992 presidential campaign without remembering Ross Perot. He enlivened the race with his humorous one-liners and creative metaphors. He took a complex issue such as dealing with the national deficit, and compared it to the crazy aunt who has been locked up in the basement and ignored. By reducing it to a simple analogy, he was able to get his point across more readily than his opponents. The humorous aspect made people listen and chuckle. Perot's biggest asset is his ability to use analogies effectively. When explaining why his partnership with General Motors didn't work, he said, "I come from an environment where if you see a snake, you kill it. These guys see a snake, get a consultant on snakes, form a committee on snakes, think about it for a year, and by the time they do anything, there are snakes all over the factory."

Maureen Dowd commented on the president's wooing of the media by saying, "Wooing the press is an exercise roughly akin to picnicking with a tiger. You might enjoy the meal, but the tiger always eats last."

Former Texas governor Ann Richards, commenting on her exercise program, related that her trainer works her harder "than a funeral-home fan in July." Sol Price, founder of Price Clubs, the forerunner of Costco/Price, was asked if he was the father of discount warehouses. Sol reportedly replied that if he were, he should have worn a condom because there were entirely too many of them. Humorous analogies are excellent ways to make your point persuasively. Want to describe a critic? He is a guy who knows the way, but can't drive a car.

Explaining occupations

Another good example of using an analogy to make your point was in a debate about NAFTA, the North American Free Trade Agreement. Speaking in opposition, one of the parties said it was "like wife-swapping with a bachelor." I offer a similar story to define consultants. I tell my audience that I once had a tom cat who would spent his evenings chasing females and enjoying the fruits of debauchery. But there was a lot of noise involved. I got tired of all the racket and had him spayed. Now, I explain, he still goes out every night, but he's now functioning as a consultant. Even consultants laugh at this.

Incidentally, it is a good idea to avoid telling lawyer jokes to attorneys. First, they've probably heard them. Second, they usually don't think they're funny. And, as I mentioned previously, they don't seem to have a very well developed sense of humor anyway. Most people think accountants and engineers lack a sense of humor but my experience has been otherwise. They do, however, seem to appreciate cerebral wit rather than broad slapstick comedy.

Endearing yourself to the audience

One last thought on using humorous analogies — the same rules apply as with any other type of humor. Be mindful of the AT&T dictum (appropriate, timely, tasteful). Public relations consultant Kathy Kerchner tells about an NFL executive who, in fielding questions about refurbishing an old stadium, said, "You can take an old broad and give her a facelift, good cosmetics and dye her hair, but she's still an old broad." The comment was seen as sexist and offensive to women.

Using a humorous metaphor not only allows you to make your point but, because it is delivered on the wings of humor, endears you to your audience. You make your point more effectively because you create a word picture to make the brain accept and digest your message more easily than a mere statement. For example, when a public figure said he had no inkling of the nefarious activities going on within his organization, a critic likened it to the fellow playing the piano in a brothel who claims not to know what is going on upstairs. This humorous analogy was much more effective than just challenging his contention.

You'll notice that good communicators regularly use metaphors to get across their message. Columnist Mark Shields, a regular on the *News Hour with Jim Lehrer*, frequently uses this method of explaining his position. Making his point about the futility of an action, he compared it to "leaving the landing lights on for Amelia Earhart." And expressing the notion of a surprise in a political matter, he said it was "like finding out that Mario Cuomo is not Italian." The analogy was made even more effective because his metaphor was linked to the subject matter under discussion.

Commenting on his efforts to grapple with our national deficit, Senator Phil Gramm said, "balancing the budget is like going to heaven. Everybody wants to do it. They just don't want to do what you have to do to make the trip." Politicians are often very good communicators and use humor to make their case. Abraham Lincoln is said to have been the first president to use humor as an executive and political tool. He was noted for his use of anecdotes to illustrate his point of view.

Creating your own analogy is an art form. You think of the point you're trying to make and then imagine it in an exaggerated form — in the context of the discussion if that's possible. Think of people who epitomize the essence of what you are trying to express. Comparison is the key to developing your own humorously creative metaphor. People, places and situations are useful in coming up with a funny analogy. You may have heard the rather trite saying, "I felt about as welcome as an illegitimate child at a family picnic." This beats merely saying that you felt unwelcome.

Noticing metaphors is a way to stimulate your own development and usage. Here are some that might inspire you to think metaphorically. Read these and then try to come up with one or more of your own.

- As slow as a nudist going through a barbed-wire fence.

- Changes sides as often as a windshield wiper.

- Friendlier than a wet dog.

- As much fun as a mosquito at a blood bank.

- As much subtlety as the Great North American Glacier.

- As nervous as a cat in a room-full of rocking chairs

Discussing the wedding of Donald Trump and Marla Maples, a reporter said of Trump, "This is a guy who draws attention the way a 7-Eleven attracts loitering teens." Here again, we see a humorous comparison made to jazz up the article. It adds color, style and flair to the description. If you would like to make your point better while you enhance your image with some creative humor, try the witty analogy.

In a flap between a major airline and its union, the Airline Pilots Association used an analogy to combat a charge that they were the bad guys. They said it was as if "the lions were suing the Christians for animal abuse." Funny and effective. Try thinking funny and comparatively. For example, "*That* is to *this* as *this* would be to _____." Supermarket tabloids are to journalism what the fortune cookie is to philosophy. So the next time you want to make a point and get a smile, use an analogy, metaphor or simile.

A pocketful of ad-libs

When a professional speaker was addressing an audience and the waitress began collecting plates and silverware from the table in front of him, he didn't miss a beat. Realizing that the entire audience was aware of the distraction, he commented, "This is my wife. We work together!"

Larry is a professional speaker who once fell off the stage during his presentation. It was only about a foot so he hit the ground without getting hurt. Lying there, he said, "I'll now take questions from the floor."

Recently, I heard a speaker discussing ad-libs. He told of seeing Robin Williams — one of the really great masters of spontaneous comedy — venture into the audience with numerous ad-libs about various spectators. Then, he saw

Robin perform several weeks later. He did the same thing, using the same ad-libs although in a little different order. Similarly, a comedy writer very familiar with Sammy Davis, Jr.'s act stayed on after one show. As he mingled with the crowd he overheard people commenting on how well Sammy Davis could ad-lib — he had a comeback for just about everything. What they didn't realize— but the comedy writer knew—is most of those clever retorts were used the same way at the same point in the show every night.

You've no doubt observed the use of a clever, humorous ad-lib in the middle of a presentation and thought just how wonderful it would be to be able to think on your feet like that. When you hear someone use an ad lib during a presentation, more often than not it's one they've pulled out of their pocket. Good ad-libs are usually not spontaneous. If you make presentations, it's a good idea to have some ad libs in reserve so that when the moment arrives and you need one, it'll be there.

Sometimes it is almost impossible to anticipate an event or comment that calls for an ad-lib. Such was the case of Minnesota State Patrol Chief Roger Ledding who was erroneously introduced as "being here with his lovely wife Beverly." When Ledding got to the lectern he began, "I'm a little nervous getting up before this distinguished audience and speaking today. But I am not nearly as nervous as I will be tonight when I must go home with my wife Audrey and explain Beverly to her!" He played off the error.

Art Linkletter was host of the popular television show *Kids Say the Darndest Things*. He tells how he was often accused of scripting the dialogue for the hilarious exchanges that took place. Linkletter says they never scripted any of it. Moreover, he says, they could never have come up with anything nearly as humorous as the kids blurted spontaneously. He says they did have a few tricks to coax some candid thoughts from them. One trick was to ask the children what their mothers told them *not* to say. As Art tells it, one kid said his mother told him not to "get on national TV and tell the whole world she was pregnant." When the little boy related that, Art asked him why, commenting, "That's a wonderful thing!"

"Cause she ain't," the lad replied.

Since we can't carry a funny kid around with us, it's always good to have some ad-libs in your pocket for occasions that most frequently arise. Here are a few to commit to memory (as well as to your humor file) for use when appropriate:

When you forget a line or fact during a presentation — "Let's see, where was I?" Then move to another spot on the stage and say, "Oh yes, I was here." When you turn your back on the audience — "Pardon my back . . . For that matter, pardon my front." When you're about to take questions — "I'd like to take questions from the smokers first, since they don't have as much time left as the rest of us."

After a delayed laugh — "It took you a while, but you got it!" or "Thank you mom and dad!"

When your presentation is delayed for any appreciable time because of a microphone malfunction — "Well how do you like it so far?"

When you need to test the microphone — "Can you hear me in the back? I'm asking that because I spoke to a group not long ago and I noticed a few people straining to hear in the rear. So I asked them, 'Can you hear me in the back?' and someone hollered 'No!' and two people from the front got up and moved to the back." In the middle of a rather lengthy story — "To make a long story short — if it's not too late for that."

Or you could be describing a group that is not very bright. Rather than saying that outright, it is more effective to say, "After all, these guys aren't laid-off employees from NASA." Or, you could say, "I wasn't meeting with a committee of MENSA." It's how you say it. You can say that something is futile or you can compare it to leaving the porch lights on for Jimmy Hoffa.

Here are just a few examples:

- He could sell hams in a synagogue.

- He had the look of Joan of Arc as they lit the kindling.

- I'm looking forward to it like a proctoscopic examination.

- Like pulling up a giant plant by the roots to see if it's growing.

Now that we've explored different ways to invigorate your verbal presentation, lets look at a few fundamentals that will help you deliver any humor you decide to use.

Using cartoons

If you are delivering a presentation using slides or overheads, you are missing the boat if you don't include some cartoons. They add humor with very little effort and help make your point. But there are some elements that will facilitate this. More often than not, I see people make some very basic mistakes in using cartoons. First, they will use a cartoon that will not make a visual impact on a screen. Whenever possible, use a simple, one-panel drawing. If you do decide to use a multi-panel or strip cartoon, show the panels individually rather than as a group. That way the audience can see them clearly and follow along as the humor sinks in.

The biggest error I notice is that the character's words are left in the slide or overhead. Always take them out and deliver them orally. There are several reasons for doing it this way. Many people view cartoons backwards. They read the caption and then look at the picture. This is tantamount to listening to the punch line before hearing the setup of a joke. Helping your audience view the cartoon in the correct order will enhance their enjoyment of it. Second, you can use your voice to heighten the impact of the humor by reciting the caption with special modulation. Finally, everyone will hear the punch line at the same time, and this simultaneous experience will maximize the group's laughter.

If you make this type of presentation, be on the lookout for cartoons that depict humorous situations related to your field or topic. When you see one that you believe is funny and appropriate, cut it out and make the adjustments mentioned above before having it put on your visual aid. Of course you can draw or have someone draw your own cartoons depicting some funny anecdote related to your audience or topic. You can also use photographs of people in your organization or known to your audience and create your own caption.

When your humor isn't working

Most people avoid humor because they're afraid of being embarrassed if it doesn't work. They think, "What will I do if I deliver the punch line and the audience just sits there looking at me like a tree full of owls?" So let's see how we can reduce and virtually eliminate the risk factor and avoid falling on our faces if we don't get the yuks we expect. First, remember that ad libs, quips and other one-liners don't require or even call for laughter. Therefore, there is really no risk. If nobody laughs or even smiles, you just go on and pretend it wasn't meant to be that funny. You haven't used much of their time and so no laugh need occur.

Risk reducer number two: report rather than deliver. "Woody Allen said that he took a course in speed reading. Then, he said, he read *War and Peace*. Said, Woody, 'It's about Russia.' You don't think that's funny? Too bad; Woody Allen is usually funny." You simply reported what Woody said. It's not your line; it's his. This is the beauty of quotes. Somebody else is writing your material; you use it and give them credit. You can also attribute it to an anonymous source: "As somebody once said, '............' "

When you've taken up the audience's time and told a joke of some length, you must be prepared to *save* it if it doesn't work. This is done with savers. More often than not, savers will produce a better laugh than if the joke had worked. That's why it's called a saver; you can't lose! You've told the joke and you don't get the laugh you expected. (This will only work if no one laughs or only a very few react.) So you look around and then go to one of the small collection of saver lines you have in your pocket. What's nice about this is that the wait is necessary for the saver to work. You look up and say, "It says here: 'Pause for laughter.'"

"The saving grace of humor is that if you fail, no one is laughing at you."
— Whitney Brown

Savers

Johnny Carson, the former late night television show host, was superb at this. The reason he became the master of savers is because he used timely material for his evening monologue. The humor was almost always about something that happened very recently. It was new material; never before tested. Consequently, some of it worked and some of it didn't. So he always came prepared to save what didn't work. He would augment his savers with marvelous expressions.

Here are a few savers to use:

- Just raise your hand if you'd like that explained

- That's the kind of material that's kept me from the big time!

- Say, this is an English-speaking audience, isn't it?

- And to think, I canceled a root canal appointment to be here!

- Is this an audience or an oil painting?

Johnny used so many of these that he would occasionally break them up with a curse. That is, he would use a humorous curse *as a saver.* He'd say, "May the Merrill Lynch bull leave a portfolio on your rug." Or, "May an 80-year-old onion farmer give you mouth-to-mouth resuscitation." Johnny Carson could use these curses because of the way he related to his audiences. You will need to assess your own relationship with your audience before going to them.

You shouldn't have to use too many savers at one setting. If most of your jokes are going over poorly, take a look at their construction and delivery. Two or three savers should be more than enough, but having them will make your humor virtually risk free.

Humor is almost always appropriate if it's selected and delivered properly. There are occasions when it is almost mandatory. If you find yourself in a setting of frivolity, it will be rather difficult to deliver a message devoid of humor. Such was the case when Supreme Court Justice Stephen Breyer delivered the commencement speech before 35,000 people at Stanford University. Stanford has a reputation for numerous lighthearted antics at graduation festivities and Breyer found himself in an atmosphere where black caps and gowns were among the few serious touches. Appropriately, he included some humor in his comments. Justice Breyer told the graduates they would be called upon to ask many questions in the course of their careers. "The science graduate will ask, 'Why does that work?' the engineering graduate, 'How does it work?' the economic graduate, 'What does it cost?' and the liberal arts graduate, 'Do you want fries with your hamburger?'"

You may find yourself in a similar situation so it is important to be prepared to include humor in your remarks. When giving a speech, just try to remember that when you have the audience on the edge of their seats, they might be trying to muster the nerve to get up and go home. Go to the humor solution — it will keep them riveted to their seats!

Letters with levity

Using humor at the lectern to warm up the crowd or break the ice is widely accepted. But we rarely see the use of humor in letters and memoranda even though it works for all the same reasons.

Humor grabs or refocuses the reader's attention and helps make the point. And, as in oral communication, it relaxes the reader and builds rapport. Almost all written correspondence lends itself to some injection of wit. Witness this collection letter from a California bank concerning a long-standing overdraft: "Dear Sir: We would be most grateful if we could revert to the old system of you banking with us." The idea is to use the light touch to convey warmth and friendliness.

Once you begin to use humor and other types of attention-getters you'll start spotting them when you see them. There are books written for the purpose of finding appropriate humor and they have indexes so you can easily locate such items. For example: *20,000 Quips & Quotes* by Evan Esar and *14,000 Quips & Quotes* by E. C. McKenzie.

Quotes are especially effective in this regard because they usually have the added advantage of coming from well-known people whose names draw the reader into the item. Some lines are very flexible. For example, "Many years ago, the late Willie Sutton was asked why he robbed banks. His answer was,

'That's where the money is.'" This can be used to introduce the subject of *why anything* or it could be used to segue to a message about money or banks or questions — any of the topics mentioned or implied in the quote. Suppose you are sending a letter or conveying any message about your product or service and you want to tout the advantages or otherwise brag about it. You can preface those remarks with a quote from Dizzy Dean who said, "It ain't bragging if you can do it!" Then you would demonstrate the fact that you actually deliver on the points you want to make.

Quotations can be flexible

There are several books from which you can obtain quotes. *Best Quotations For All Occasions* by Lewis C. Henry (Fawcett Publications) is one. *The 637 Best Things Anybody Ever Said* by Robert Byrne (Fawcett Crest) has several sequels and contains numerous humorous quotes tying into various subjects and I highly recommend it. There is also a book entitled *1,001 logical Laws, Accurate Axioms, Profound Principles, Trusty Truisms, Homey Homilies, Colorful Corollaries, Quotable Quotes, and Rambunctious Ruminations For All Walks Of Life* by Peers/Bennett/Booth (Fawcett Gold Medal) which, as the title implies, is full of funny, usable items of all kinds for spicing up your communications.

Using humor will add color, style and flair to your messages. It will grease the way for your message and make them laugh while you make your point. It will ensure your readers' attention and interest. When U.S. Rep. Helen Chenoweth of Idaho wanted to get the attention of her colleagues in an effort to block the reintroduction of bears into her state, she sent them this communication: "Question: What does a grizzly bear call a hiker? Answer: Lunch."

What are the rules? There are some differences in the use of humor with oral presentations and written correspondence. For one thing, consideration must be given to the length of the item. A joke of any length would usually be out of place in a memo or letter, but might fit nicely into an oral presentation of any appreciable duration. In any case, most of the same rules apply. The humor or other spice should be, as we have discussed, AT&T (appropriate, timely and tasteful).

Segues

Another very important rule is that they should be relevant. This is also probably the trickiest too! It's hard enough to find items that are funny, but the task becomes even more difficult when the item must be tied into the subject matter. That is where segues come in.

The purpose of segues is to *make* your material relevant. It's always nice to have a funny item that meets the other tests and is especially relevant too. But more often than not, it won't be available. Therefore, you make the field of material wider by using subtopics and cleverly segueing into the selected item. The term "segue" is a relatively new term as it is being used here. It was originally a musical term but is used by speakers and other entertainers to denote bridging or transitioning from one point to another in a smooth or unnoticed manner. Let's see how this works. We need to start with a humor item and work backwards.

Here's an item I recently saw: "We all admire the wisdom of people who come to us for advice." The quote was attributed to a Jack Herbert. I don't know who he is so I won't assume others do and thus won't use his name in a prominent manner as I might if he were well-known. I can use this statement to tie into the topics of admiration, wisdom, advice, ego and knowledge.

Where to find the items? Newspapers, magazines and television are good places to find material. A more obvious place to look is the joke book. But there are thousands of these and it is possible to waste a lot of time unless you follow a couple of steps in gathering material from them. First, the kind of book you'll want to peruse depends on how you plan to use the humor.

If you're planning on using it in rather lengthy speeches, then the regular joke book will do fine. If, on the other hand, you plan to use the material in letters and memos, you'll want to concentrate on finding quips & quotes and other forms of brief humor. In any case, check the book you initially choose to be certain you find the material funny. You'll be surprised how these books break down into two groups; those you find humorous and those you don't.

Mark the funny stuff

As we discussed in chapter two, a joke book is not read the same as other books. You must read it in spurts. If you read more than about fifteen minutes at one time, you will lose your perspective on what is desirable. I suggest you mark the book with a check mark when you find an item you want to save. If it's a borrowed book, you can use the 3M post-its to temporarily identify material you want to keep. Then after you've accumulated enough to post for your own use, either copy them off to 3 x 5 cards or put them into your computer. When you do enter them into your file, identify all the subtopics and cross-index them by subtopic as well.

One of the mistakes people make when trying to tie in humor to their presentations or other message is to assume you need a "joke." More often than not, a short quip, quote or one-liner will do better than a standard joke. There are several reasons for this. Besides the fact that you'll usually want something brief to fit into your message, there is the ROI (return on investment) rule to consider. The length of time you take to deliver your humor should be equivalent to the result you attain in terms of laughter or other appreciation. A standard joke is expected to yield more laughter than a quip or one-liner. In fact, if the latter fails to get a laugh in an oral presentation, you can simply go on as though it was only meant to elicit a smile.

Summary

Humor can be used to strengthen almost any form of communication, from group presentations and personal conversations to business letters. Building humor into your written communications will energize and reinforce them in many ways. Perhaps most importantly, humor closes the gap between speaker/writer and listener/reader by building an emotional bridge. It's hard to overstate the value of this point. The purpose of most communications is to persuade. It is difficult, if not impossible to be persuaded by someone you don't like. Can you imagine buying a product or an idea from a person you dislike? And can you imagine laughing with this person? Use all the various tools to enhance your communications. Just as an artist uses many different colors, so you will be more effective drawing on different elements of theater to strengthen your persuasive powers and hammer home your message. Remember: your messages will fly better if you send them on the wings of humor.

Sign at a company eating area: Please clean up after yourself Your mother doesn't live here!

Chapter Five

Bring Joy to Your Job and Wit to the Workplace

The fact that most people die between eight o'clock and nine o'clock on Monday mornings is a way of saying, "I hate my job; I'm outta here!" People who arrive at work with such negative feelings will never excel at their jobs.

It is difficult to overstate the importance of joy and good feelings in producing excellence. During an NFL football game, Denver Broncos kicker Rich Karlis was called on to kick a field goal with the game on the line. Coach Dan Reeves took a time out. He called Karlis aside and told him to take a moment to sit down and visualize his previous year's field goal that won the game and took the team to the Super Bowl. Said Reeves, "Relive that moment. Feel the joy you felt then." Karlis put the ball through the uprights.

Every organization seeks excellence. But what are the elements that comprise this valuable attribute? We know that excellence is almost always the result of a great deal of energy and effort. What we often forget is that it is even more the product of enthusiasm, excitement and exhilaration. Energy and effort are physical. Enthusiasm, excitement and exhilaration are products of the mind and involve our emotions, impulses and passions.

Employees who are enthusiastic and excited about their jobs will have more fun at the office and will be less likely to grouse about long hours. They are the people who will expend more energy and effort; and will know the exhilaration of a job well done. You can buy a dog and you can teach it tricks. But you cannot teach a dog to wag its tail. That's something that comes with trust, respect, likability and other traits that are earned. It is the same with employees.

The benefits

Some people come to work with the same level of enthusiasm they'd have for being attacked by a pack of hungry jackals. Putting humor, fun and play into your job or organization is a way of injecting excitement and enthusiasm into the workplace. It is but one major aspect of creating a "nice place to work." But the results are more than altruistic. There is ample evidence that humor at work pays off for the employer in dollars and cents.

Franklin Research and Development took a look at those companies listed in *The Best 100 Companies to Work for in America*, a book by Robert Levering and Milton Moskowitz. They analyzed the seventy public companies and found they were twice as profitable as the average Standard & Poor 500 company and that their stock prices grew at three times the average rate. Levering reports, "Companies are realizing that they can't deliver on the bottom line if they can't deliver a work force that feels happy and comfortable." The authors looked at the many ways companies use different methods to make their firms successful but concluded that once in a while employees just gotta have fun! They cited Ben & Jerry's, the maker of politically correct ice cream, as taking the cake in the fun department. The company holds an annual Elvis Day, featuring — what else — peanut butter and marshmallow sandwiches. It also has an official "minister of joy" who once distributed cardboard figures of the face of former CEO Fred Lager. The purpose: A "Disfigure Fred's Head" contest. According to their study, a pleasant workplace is related to corporate success.

A spirited environment

Tom Peters, coauthor of *In Search of Excellence*, says that excellence is the result of a "spirited environment," which he defines as one marked with laughter, enthusiasm for being on the team and a willingness to do just about anything to make the service or product better. Let's look at some ways we can use the humor solution to create that spirited environment. What will happen if you instill humor, fun and play into the workplace? When properly ingrained into the corporate culture, it will increase production, encourage creativity, energize the workforce and create a sense of passion that can translate into organizational success.

This is not as simple as it sounds. It involves adjusting your organizational culture to ensure that there is an open environment where employees feel empowered and trust reigns throughout the workplace. Before you try to use the ideas and techniques mentioned here, it is important to be certain your organization has the proper environment. Otherwise, these techniques will backfire.

Just as most plant life requires the proper soil, climate and care to grow, the spirited work environment needs a proper atmosphere in which to flourish. In other words, humor, fun and play cannot be plopped into just any work milieu and be expected to have the desired effect.

Appropriate management style

Trust is an important part of any organization or team. If members don't trust each other it's pretty much impossible to get a team effort. There is an inverse relationship between trust and tension. When one is up, the other is automatically down. Like a teeter totter, they counterbalance each other. If trust does not prevail in your organization, that is the first problem to be solved. Trust must exist between the team members and the leadership. For employees to feel empowered, an appropriate management style must be in place. "Participative management" simply means the employees must have a meaningful say in decision-making.

Part of that package is a low level of open dissension. John Sculley, former CEO of Apple Computer, used to say that dissension is like arsenic; a little bit is healthy, but a lot of it will kill you. There should be room for differences of opinion and it should be okay to disagree. Diplomats who served in Baghdad tell the story about one of Saddam Hussein's cabinet meetings. Saddam asked his ministers if any of them had a contrary view of one of his proposals. Only one minister spoke up. Saddam thanked him graciously and invited him to discuss it further in his private office. Inside, he beat the man to death with a club.

I have a close friend who works for a department of the State of California that recently underwent reorganization. Following the implementation of the various new procedures, supervisors were called together and asked to write down all the things that were not working or that needed improvement. They did. At the next meeting those who complied were given reprimands for being negative, uncooperative and resisting change. The message to employees was clear: We don't tolerate disagreement, dissension or even constructive criticism — even when we ask for it!

As my colleague, Bob Basso likes to say, an environment perceived as threatening is not conducive to the free flow of information. In the above environment, there will be no free flow of information. Management is not likely to get the pulse of the organization again.

"The number one premise of business is that it need not be boring or dull. It ought to be fun. If it's not fun, you're wasting your life."
— Tom Peters

Empowerment

Empowerment doesn't mean turning over complete responsibility to your team. It does mean giving them some reasonable measure of control over their own professional lives. It has taken on a wide range of employee involvement in management decisions, up to and including "open-book management." The term refers to a company's complete openness with employees about its financial status, projections, costs, expenses and even salaries. Employees attend regular meetings and workshops to track the progress of the company. It is becoming more and more popular and helps employees feel, think and act like owners.

One of my best clients is Hewlett Packard. I'm always impressed with this company every time I have the opportunity to work with them. When they have a meeting, someone is put in charge of getting the speakers and given the necessary authority. In most companies I've worked with, the person assigned the task is required to check with supervisors at several levels for approval.

"If you are too busy to laugh, you are too busy."
— Bob Ross

During one of my visits to Hewlett-Packard an employee was telling me about Lew Platt, the CEO. He was asked to write an article for the company's newsletter. He agreed and told the editor he would submit it by a certain date. When the deadline arrived, the CEO went to the editor's office, asked to be admitted and requested additional time, explaining that he had fallen behind because of some other pressing business. This story was related to me by a mid-level manager to illustrate the egalitarian attitude of their CEO. The point, as he explained it, is that the CEO could have called the editor, ignored the deadline, sent an underling or a note and could have simply told the editor his submission would be late. Instead, he took the time to appear in person, apologize, and request additional time. Without any other information, what does this tell you about Mr. Platt and his leadership style?

Empowered employees motivated by fun and play can come up with incredible ideas that can be turned into productivity and profit. Take the case of Formulabs, a 48-year-old international company based in Escondido, California, that manufacturers commercial ink. They recently decided to tap the creativity of their work force. They staged an internal competition to improve operations. Bruce Nichols, president and CEO purposely kept the rules loose. To reinforce the fun aspect of the program, called Q-Tip (for Quality Teams for Improved Performance) a Western theme was adopted with teams taking on such names as the Posse, the Buffalo Chips and the Donner Party.

> *"Real success is finding your lifework in the work that you love."*
> — David McCullough

When they announced the results at a Western "roundup," it was beyond what they had expected. The winning team, called the Desperadoes, consisting of five employees from marketing and technical departments laid out a new plan for an innovative type of printing process that could become a new business line for the company. The contest was so successful that another one is already being planned — this one with a beach theme.

Brian O'Shaughnessy, President and CEO of Revere Copper Products, bought the firm from previous owners who had hired him as their CEO after they had done a leveraged buy-out of the company. One of the first things he did after taking ownership was to begin giving it away. He gave every employee a small share in the company. He extracted no quid pro quo; it was just a gift and an effective way of saying that he wanted each employee to have a piece of the action.

Creativity

One of the biggest advantages of an empowered workforce is a workplace where creativity flourishes. A manager who is not tapping the creativity of the employees is missing out on a major resource. One of the best ways of expressing creativity was demonstrated at an Israeli high school. Before they were given a standard creativity test, 141 tenth-graders were treated to a recording of a popular comedian. Those who heard it did significantly better than the control group, which was not so entertained. Humor can show us the ambiguity of situations, revealing non-standard and often startling answers.

Stimulating creativity in a corporate — or other organizational — culture means setting up the correct climate. John Sculley, former top executive of Pepsi and Apple Computers says, "Creative people require the tools and environment that foster their success. Above all, they require an atmosphere conducive to fun and to thinking in non-standard ways. The work environment needs to be informal and relaxed."

In addition, encouraging creativity means a high tolerance for failure — even a celebration of it. The absence of failure means there is a lack of new ideas and experimentation. It is similar to the banking industry. When there are no loan defaults, it signifies that underwriting standards are too restrictive. If you want an abundance of creativity you must have a healthy tolerance for failure. A humorous atmosphere helps too.

Scientists at Monsanto Company's research laboratories learned from humor consultants to press nickels into their foreheads and then drop them into a cup. Some of the scientists report a fifty percent surge in creativity after doing the nickel stunt. Such silliness seems to stimulate creative thinking.

"Work is love made visible."

— Kahlil Gibran

Before discussing the various ways of bringing joy to the workplace, let's look at a company that has had tremendous success in building a corporate culture full of fun through a system called "management by fooling around."

Southwest Airlines has been incredibly successful at harnessing the power of humor. And they have received lots of free publicity in the process, probably because the methods used to put fun and play into every aspect of their operation are so outrageous. They have been hailed for their vivacity and the fact that they may be the only major U.S. company that actually *requires* a sense of humor.

The pace is set at the top

Let me emphasize that this is not just some kooky, offbeat firm. The Dallas-based airline has risen to the top in one of the country's most fiercely competitive and cutthroat industries. It is the nation's fifth largest air carrier and shows up on list after list of the best-run companies in America. Over the past 25 years, it has grown from 198 employees to 24,000. The fooling around starts right at the top with CEO Herb Kelleher. What other top corporate executive do you know who dresses up like Elvis Presley or the Easter Bunny and parades around an airport? He sets the pace and it's picked up all the way down the line.

In fact, the fooling around doesn't stop with employees. Customers get in on the act too — with encouragement from the fun-loving crews. Contests are sometimes held on flights to see which passenger has the biggest hole in a sock. On Halloween, customers are made up to look like Dracula, complete with fangs and fake blood stains.

Fooling around has made Southwest Airlines one of the giants of the industry. And it has turned a profit for more than 20 years — a record unmatched by its competitors. SWA also has the lowest employee turnover and the best labor relations in the industry. The secret of their success is having a highly productive workforce motivated by a passion for their jobs. The employees believe their mission is to provide travel, in the form of inexpensive fares, to those who could not otherwise afford it.

But Southwest Airlines is not all horseplay. This is productive fun! Herb Kelleher serves as an example, not only for having fun, but for his devotion to the business, his energy and his commitment to the employees. That's probably why SWA has the highest record of on-time arrivals and the lowest number of customer complaints.

As many successful companies are finding, the foundation for prosperity is the employees. At SWA customer service is a by-product of employee devotion. They have a saying that the customer is *not* always right. The employee comes first. They believe their attitude ultimately translates into a good customer relations program.

This is a philosophy shared by such companies as Disney and Federal Express. Around the Disney workplace you won't find the word "employee." Instead, they are referred to as "cast," and you'll see signs that read: "Cast Activities, Cast News." They have a saying: "You get good performance on-stage if you take care of your cast backstage."

This same fundamental principle is at work at Federal Express where senior vice-president James Perkins believes if you take care of your own people, they will deliver service and products in an efficient and courteous manner. The statistics prove him right. In 15 years, that firm has grown to a $4 billion company and is listed as one of the top ten in *The 100 Best Companies To Work For In America*. It is the mirror effect about which John Naisbitt writes, "You can't have good customer relations if you have poor employee relations."

Cultural shock

Potential Southwest Airlines employees view a film about the company, so they know what to expect. Can you imagine new employees coming from a traditional, stodgy workplace? They must go into cultural shock when they find out the CEO is called "Big Daddy-O" and see him doing a rap song about the company. ("My name is Herb, Big Daddy-O. I run this show. Without your help, there'd be no love. On the ground below or in the air above!") Employees are steeped in this upbeat corporate philosophy and learn that the idea is to set up an atmosphere that makes them excited about coming to work, makes it fun to be at work and encourages people to have a good time and enjoy themselves. They even have a "culture committee" of 100 employees to install and maintain the proper spirit within their organization.

Their approach to virtually all situations is to look to the humor solution. When Northwest Airlines ran an ad stating that they were number one in customer satisfaction, SWA knew they were off base and some wanted to sue to stop the ad. But cooler and more humorous minds prevailed. SWA ran an ad responding to Northwest that referenced their ad and read: "Liar, liar, pants on fire!"

If you've seen any of Southwest Airlines' advertising, you've probably noticed their slogan is, "Just Plane Smart." It was only after they began using this slogan that they discovered it might have been inadvertently plagiarized. It seems that a small aviation company in Greenville, South Carolina, had come up with it first. What to do? In almost every similar case, the parties would contact their attorneys and take to the courts for a protracted and expensive legal battle. But this was not any other company.

So, it is not surprising that the parties decided that this dispute could best be settled by a little foolishness. They agreed to arm wrestle for the right to use the slogan. Southwest's Kelleher volunteered to represent his company and arm wrestle the larger, younger and obviously stronger opponent. While this fellow trained in a gym by pumping iron, the chain-smoking Kelleher was videotaped lifting two bottles of Wild Turkey (bourbon). When showdown time came, it took place in a wild atmosphere reminiscent of professional wrestling. A large group of shapely cheerleaders, recruited from the company's flight attendants, led the encouragement for outclassed Herb. A referee wearing a horrible orange wig officiated. Proceeds from ticket sales went to charity. Poor Herb's arm was downed without much resistance. The Wild Turkey regimen hadn't worked as well as traditional weight lifting.

In the end, though, it all came out well as Southwest Airlines was given — in spite of the loss — the right to use the slogan. Besides all the fun, the contestant firms calculated that they saved in excess of a half million dollars in legal fees.

Inventory of fun

Companies are coming up with all sorts of ways to make a pleasant work environment and, through that enjoyable environment, communicate that they really care about their employees. Lindsay Collier, an executive with Eastman Kodak Company, felt the firm needed to lighten up so he commissioned a "humor task force" and gave them the assignment of building a "humor room" at the company's Rochester, New York, headquarters. It was stocked with funny videos, books and gag items such as plastic hamburgers and windup chattering teeth. When the company decided to downsize, he circulated a memo playing off the release of a movie that coincided with the event— "Honey, I Shrunk The Company."

Sprint Corporation organized a Fun At Work day and brought together 3,000 workers at regional offices nationwide. Divided into teams, they raced to see who could take the zaniest photos of themselves. Margery Tippen, the Sprint executive who arranged the company-sponsored laughs, said, "We believe employees who have fun feel appreciated and come together as a team. That helps them be more productive and helps our customers."

Companies across the country are finding ways to make use of the power of humor, fun and play to foster cooperation and teamwork among their employees. Corporate America is spending an increasing amount of time and money to put employees into challenges outside the office in hopes of realizing cohesion, collaboration and camaraderie when they get back to work. FCC National Bank of Wilmington, Delaware, sent seven of its senior managers to a Manhattan cooking school. The idea was to turn them loose in the kitchen with instructions and ingredients for a gourmet lunch. With incomplete instructions, participants found themselves needing to improve on giving and accepting feedback.

Fun in the course of change

Cosmetics giant Estee Lauder sent its entire sales promotion department out of their Fifth Avenue office and into the Central Park Conservancy's Professional Development Program for a day of team-building and leadership exercises on the lush park grounds. It involved discussions and games, races and rock climbing. Hollywood studio executives rafted down the Colorado River in a similar exercise.

Versatec is a company that gives out annual bonuses — but not in the usual way. It employs some of the aspects of show business. President and CEO Renn Zaphiropoulous arrived at one such award ceremony riding on an elephant alongside a marching band and dressed in a colorful costume.

I work with numerous organizations to help them build a spirited work environment. While injecting some good-natured fun into the atmosphere is almost always appropriate, it is even more crucial when they are in the midst of substantial change. San Diego Gas & Electric was recently merged with a company called Enova. The merger wrought chaos among the utility company's marketing staff. As in any such consolidation, everyone anticipated the downsizing that was sure to occur.

Sales slumped and progress toward sales goals was only a fraction of what it should have been. They gathered their marketing people together and brought me in masquerading as a special assistant to the CEO of the new parent company. I delivered a wacky message and told them they would be required to have a standard, canned sales pitch. I explained that their new boss was previously with a real estate company fond of uniform company blazers. I then displayed the most garish sports coat I could find complete with their new logo. This and other parts of the message got them laughing as a group and put the situation in perspective. After lunch they got together for a team sand castle building exercise. Fun and play was the fare for the day with the hopeful result of fostering enthusiasm, exhilaration and esprit de corps back on the job.

On those occasions when you do get the work team together for some fun, always take photos for posterity. I was visiting a friend who worked at the offices of Tony Robbins. As I waited for him in the guest area I picked up a photo album from a table and found page after page of pictures of the work force partying together. Tony was right there and the fun was preserved and relived through the magic of photography.

If your job is being the boss, you might want to consider doing it differently and with fun. A manager who has a basketball hoop over his wastebasket and a humorous sign on his desk is viewed by his employees much differently than a no-nonsense type of manager with a traditional office setting. If you have a special assignment for one of your team members, try doing an audio tape along the lines of the *Mission Impossible* instructions. Have a magic wand on your desk and when people ask you to do the impossible, pick it up and wave it.

Dress-down day

Also known by such sobriquets as "grub day," "jeans day," and "casual Friday," these days are thought to have had their origin at Hewlett Packard when Friday was the day products were shipped. When they had a backlog of goods to go out, all workers would come to work dressed casually so they could help with the shipping. The practice spread when HP employees were hired by other Silicon Valley companies. Today, relaxed dress codes are legendary among high-tech firms in that area.

Apple Computer was one of the leading trend setters in this area. Earlier CEOs such as Steve Jobs and John Scully normally came to work in blue jeans. This was in stark contrast to their main competitor, IBM, where specific dress was expected, including blue shirt and red tie. There is a funny story about the occasion when a meeting was scheduled between these two computer giants to discuss a common project. The folks at IBM told their management group that, in deference to the casual dress code at Apple, they should relax their own form of dress for this meeting. At Apple, their group was reminded of the formal style of IBM and it was suggested that they dress up for the event. When the meeting occurred, the two teams met in a dress type that was the reverse of their respective styles.

Also common in Silicon Valley are the Friday "beer busts" regularly sponsored by companies so employees can come together in a relaxed atmosphere to discuss discoveries and achievements of the week. Through this productive party, management is saying, "We care about you!"

According to its proponents, a beer bust has such ancillary effects as promoting informality among people. This practice is not confined to high-tech or even manufacturing operations. Even normally stodgy attorneys have gotten in on the act. A Menlo Park, California, law firm has adopted a variation of the practice. They have a ice cream break at 3 o'clock in the afternoon.

Besides such things as "dress-down day," companies are finding other ways to create positive work places such as free day-care and two-dollar haircuts at the company barber shop — on company time. Other such amenities all add festivity and a sense of caring to the work place. G.E. put score boards conspicuously around the plant during the World Series as one subtle but effective way of saying "we care."

> *"Don't let dogged determination kill your sense of fun.*
> *An element of playfulness will make you more creative,*
> *more satisfied and, yes, more productive, too."*
>
> —Psychology Today

Party! Celebrate everything! Have a Christmas party in July; sponsor a chili cook-off; find any way you can to gather your people together for some fun. Decorate offices and meeting rooms with humorous pictures, posters and cartoons. Be sure to capture your organizational parties on film so you can relive and celebrate them vicariously again and again.

Sun Microsystems, a California-based computer company, stages an elaborate ruse each year on April Fool's Day, usually at the expense of upper management. One year, employees took apart a vice president's office and reassembled it, afloat, on a nearby fish pond. Another year, they built a three-hole golf course in the chairman's office.

Some other events used by different companies — silly hat contest, weird shoe and crazy tie competition. One company I read about took the collection of ties from such a contest, cut them up and put them on the wall as decorations as well as a commemoration of the event. Another idea is to have an Aloha Day where employees come to work wearing Hawaiian casual dress during winter days. Put up a humor bulletin board to attract cartoons, funny articles, baby photos and jokes. Bank of America held a joke of the day contest. It ended up publishing a book of the employee's best one-liners.

Nullifying rumors

National Computer Systems of Minneapolis hired an "Elation Strategist" to "lighten up the joint." The idea was to help people relieve stress and help supervisors become better communicators and managers. Other companies have made similar efforts to lighten up their work forces by creating a "Lite Brigade," charged with coming up with ideas for injecting humor, fun and play. The company that makes Ben & Jerry's Ice Cream has a "Joy Gang" whose purpose is to plan and implement a variety of joyful activities and events throughout the year. Try designating an "In-house psychiatrist" to interpret and explain screwy procedures, events and situations. If your place is replete with rumors, try having a "rumor center" to collect contrived as well as actual rumors for dissemination.

Digital Equipment took a reverse approach. They established a "Grouch Patrol" to spot anybody slamming a phone or snapping a pencil. When someone was caught in such a negative act, they would get a "bat face" from a fellow employee. Bat faces were taught to them by humor consultant C.W. Metcalf. He also instituted a "humor support group" to create an inventory of pleasant experiences and to help humor-impaired employees enjoy the workplace and have fun at least once a month.

One company has a bimonthly Mismatch Day in which they try to wear the worst possible combinations of clothes. People show up with lots of polka dots and plaids. Another organization has company picnics with dunking booths where managers and supervisors are dunked in a fun atmosphere. The money raised goes to local charities.

These activities often have practical purposes beyond invigorating the work force. Scott Gibson, president of Sequent Computer Systems, a Beaverton, Oregon, computer manufacturing company, has a humorous approach to reducing comments critical of his company's customers. He placed 100 boxes with a picture of Bozo the clown in conference rooms, hallways and other conversation spots around his firm. Anyone caught by a fellow employee criticizing a customer or a supplier was required to drop a quarter in the nearest Bozo Box. Proceeds went to the needy and employees were kept aware of the importance of customer service.

Green light for humor

Similarly, Intel Corporation has a special prize to chastise executives who make boneheaded comments to the media. It is a leather dog muzzle mounted on a wooden plaque and called "The Muzzle Award." Companies such as Manville Corp., Safeway Stores and Northwestern Bell Telephone have instituted a number of humor programs to help employees unwind. Many firms have made their break rooms into "humor rooms." Some have installed a kiosk to encourage employees to post cartoons and other funny items.

The idea is to foster a corporate culture that encourages humor, fun and play. If you're the big potato in the organization, you can't be expected to orchestrate all these activities. Your job is primarily to "put up the green lights." Your speeches, reports and memoranda should reflect this attitude. Everybody can't be Southwest's Herb Kelleher but you can create the proper atmosphere.

The message is clear. Drill-sergeant management is on the way out. The "plantation mentality" is passé. Participative management is alive and well and thriving. This is apparent when examining such companies as General Electric, the second largest corporation in America. Their annual report of several years ago states it quite precisely in a message from John Welsh, Chairman of the Board and CEO: "We want [employees] to go home from work wanting to talk about what they did that day, rather than trying to forget about it. We want factories where the whistle blows and someone suddenly wonders aloud why we need a whistle. We want a company where people find a better way, every day, of doing things, and where, by shaping their own work experience, they make their lives better and [our] Company best." The report adds: "Farfetched? Fuzzy? Soft? Naive? Not a bit. This is the type of liberated, involved, excited, boundary-less culture that is present in successful start-up enterprises. It is unheard of in an institution our size; but we want it and we are determined we will have it."

Create your own holiday

A friendly workplace is not a passing trend. It is part of the "information age" in which we find ourselves. And since the "people approach," sometimes called "warm-wear," is based on human nature, we can expect to see it around for a long time. Yes, there is ample evidence that the punchline can affect the bottom line.

So if you'd like to energize your workplace, try establishing a Teddy Day — the name one company gives to the day they select and honor the employee who has helped his or her fellow employees the most during the past year. Hold

101

a cartoon contest or even a competition to come up with the best way to introduce fun into your work environment.

Every month, every week and virtually every day is designated as something. Use some of these as catalysts for instilling a sense of fun on the job. January has National Popcorn Day (January 27). How about popcorn for everyone? Employees love pleasant surprises. It is also the birthday of Levi Strauss, the blue jean man — an excellent day to go casual. If you don't have casual days, it's a good time to kick off such a program! February holds Northern Hemisphere Hodie Hoo Day. So have a contest or exhibition of hoodieing your hoo. What is it? Have the employees come up with the answer.

During the month of March, we celebrate Television Turn-Off Week and National Pet Sitters Week. Why not have a contest for naming the worst television program, or have a "bring your pet to work day/week." Or put the whole thing off. After all, it's National Procrastination Week too! March 26 is Make Up Your Own Holiday Day. This is a great time to have employees suggest their own original holiday. The company may even want to select one to celebrate. Then, on March 27, we celebrate the day the urinal was invented. Here's an idea. Hang a sign in the restroom that commemorates this significant occasion! This is followed by March 29, which is Teacher Appreciation Day. Employees could be asked to write a short article about their own most memorable teacher. It could be put in the company newsletter or on a bulletin board for other employees to enjoy. March is National Pothole Month, so if your company is desirous of a little publicity, you could have employees identify their favorite pothole for repair and send the city the money to do the restoration. Let the local newspaper know about it — it's the kind of thing they love to mention. So you can see that with a little imagination you can take the various offbeat holidays and make them into workplace fun.

Good-natured fun

April, for example, is National Humor Month and National Anxiety Month among others. What a great time to celebrate humor, or, if you prefer, anxiety. "What is your greatest anxiety" contest. The month begins with April Fool's Day — a natural for having some good-natured fun. It is also National Fun at Work Day! April 5 is Lady Luck Day as well as Plan Your Epitaph Day. Have employees write their own epitaphs! It is also Recycling Month and National Poetry Month. Opportunities abound for innovative fun and stress reduction. June holds National Morticians' Day and National Splurge Day as well as (attention all you Three Stooges fans) the Moe Howard Centennial — the 100th birthday of the guy with the bad haircut. You ought to be able to do something with at least one of these.

July 3 marks the beginning of "Dog Days." Use that to hold a "bring your pet to work day" (if you haven't done it in March). One company does this annually and conducts a "pet trick contest" in conjunction with it. One year the fellow who won brought his dog to the office and gave the command, "Wander." July is also Anti-Boredom Month and contains American Redneck Day.

August is National Psychic Month. Why not have employees make predictions and give a prize to the most imaginative. Or, what about a prize for the wackiest prediction? In August we'll also find Bad Poetry Day. Here is an opportunity to have team members see who can come up with the worst poem.

October gives us Pet Peeve Week and there is an International Moment of Frustration Scream Day (honest — October 12). The point is that, with some minimal thinking, these are great fodder for fun days or clusters of days. It is also when we'll find National Obnoxious Day. Who can come up with the most innovative way or the most effective way of being obnoxious to customers or fellow employees. October is a great month for some timely frivolity. It holds "Getting the World to Beat a Path to Your Door Week." Ask employees what is the best and most innovative way to do that. Have a contest!

Another day is "Be Bald and Be Free Day." Honor the baldest of the bald among your group! The very next day is "National Grouch Day." Indulge, describe or identify your favorite curmudgeon. That's followed by "Evaluate Your Life Day." How do your people evaluate the quality of their lives? Find out. That same date is also the day (in 1987) when the Dow Jones Industrial Average plunged 508 points. Use that opportunity to ferret out your teams' favorite investments. The examples are limitless!

Provide a humungous jar of peanut butter during November (Peanut Butter Lover's Month). A magician performing at lunchtime on National Magic Day or finger sandwiches taken around and given out in mid-morning on Sandwich Day in November would be appropriate.

You can use one or more of the above ideas or use this list of unusual days, weeks and months and a little imagination to come up with lots of novel ideas for injecting some of your own humor, fun and play into the work environment.

One of the questions asked of me when I'm extolling the virtues of having fun at work is, what to do if you're not the boss and can't set the stage for this kind of an atmosphere. I always tell them to just light up their corner. Unless your boss or the organizational culture forbids fun in your workplace, you are always free to brighten up your team with mirth. My advice is to light up your own little corner and stand back. People tend to gravitate to fun-filled environments.

103

Send a signal

You have to send clear signals that it's okay to have fun at work. This can be done overtly as well as covertly. Signs, posters and pictures are excellent ways of communicating. Consider these two offices; one has a list of the company's rules on its wall, while the other has a blown-up cartoon posted. They both provide clues to the occupant's character and personality. Likewise, the letters and memos emanating from your office reflect your sense of humor and attitude about the workplace.

Humor is the lubricating oil of business. It prevents friction and wins good will. It is not without some risk, though. My friend Bob was a top store manager for one of the large supermarket chains. His store was always in the top three of the chain's thirty-eight southern California stores. They were consistently profitable and high volume. He was one of the very best they had. The supermarket top brass would compliment Bob but admonish him for his management style.

You see, he liked having fun on the job and his employees enjoyed working. Bob attributed employee morale and productivity to this fun attitude. So Bob's boss would tell him that he's doing a great job — as evidenced by the numbers — but that he should try not to have fun; he should take his job more seriously and do away with the laughter, fun and play. Bob's response: "That's why I do well wherever you put me!" His boss' reaction: "Yes, but just think how much better you'd do if you eliminated that attitude."

The case (a real one!) illustrates the problem with those who are not attuned to this philosophy and who remain committed to the old "have your fun someplace else" attitude. The problem for the chain was that employees of other stores wanted to work at Bob's place. The company wouldn't tell Bob that having fun was against the rules, but they would make snide remarks such as "we're going to break up this happy family you have." Bob continued to manage with humor, fun and play and survived by pointing to the bottom line. It's not easy to use humor in the workplace if you are swimming against the tide.

Silicon Valley is a place where a fun-filled work environment is not frowned upon but is actually encouraged. They thrive on their employees' commitment, creativity and input. The fun goes across hierarchical lines. In one instance, an executive's fellow employees filled his office completely with balloons on his birthday. On another such occasion, a top staff took a Volkswagen and disassembled it, then reassembled it in their colleague's office.

A little less dramatic and more frequent practical joke is to play games with someone who has a goldfish bowl. You buy different size fishes and if they have a very small one, you replace the fish every day or so, gradually increasing its size so that the owner believes the fish is growing in leaps and bounds. Then, when you get to your biggest fish, you reverse the process so they think the fish is shrinking. This can be done in either order, depending upon what size fish you start with.

Foundation for excellence

Whether you are managing yourself or others, always remember that everyone performs better if they enjoy what they're doing. When you are performing at less than your potential, revert to fun. If you can figure out how to make it fun, your performance will improve dramatically. In the seventh and final game if the 1997 World Series, the Cleveland Indians surprised a lot of folks in selecting 21-year-old rookie, Jaret Wright, to be their pitcher. When he was interviewed before the game, Wright said, "I'm going to make it fun and have a good time." Although the Indians lost the game and the Series, Wright delivered a marvelous performance. As his team manager said, "Jaret was outstanding — gave us everything we wanted and then some." This is a recurring theme in all sports. New football coaches know their first task is to "make it fun." Why? Because it is the foundation for excellence. People do not excel out of drudgery.

The bottom line is if you're not tapping your employees' human potential, you're wasting the most precious asset you have. Making the workplace pleasant and the job fun will make your company a success. As colleague Bob Basso

says: "If your employees are coming to work with the attitude that it's their punishment for not marrying rich, there is no way you are going to get the excellence, creativity, customer service and other successful traits you seek."

In these days of mergers, buy-outs, downsizing, rightsizing and other such corporate "adjustments" the only real job security anyone actually has is their own set of job skills. And in this set of skills, the most important, by far, is "people skills." Success at any level and in almost any setting has more to do with dealing with people effectively than anything else.

Jest for the health of it

An interesting postscript to humor in the workplace is the issue of stress. The primary source of stress in the lives of most people is their job. It seems to be a by-product of the normal work environment. A bad day at the office can raise a worker's blood pressure and inflict other stress-related maladies. While most people don't have an established method of dealing with job-related stress — or any other stress for that matter, it is wise to adopt one.

The Japanese are faced with an inordinate amount of stress. According to a 1992 study on worker health, the Ministry of Labor finds that six of every ten employees feel "strong stress" on the job. Most of it is due to problems with co-workers and heavy work loads. Frustrated by a straitlaced society, the Japanese are seeking unique ways of handling it. The most common form for letting off steam is a long drinking bout after work. But many are now visiting a newly established "relief room" in Yamanakako, a lakeside vacation town at the foot of Mount Fiji. They are paying 10,000 yen (about $80) to break porcelain vases, ceramic ware and other antiques. The place is basically a four-story fun house full of fragile wares that the owner buys in bulk loads. His customers scream and yell as they hurl items against the wall — often berating tyrannical bosses and unfaithful loved ones — in two-hour sessions. The stress melts away.

Greatness will come with fun

Kobe Bryant is a promising new basketball star. He's being touted as the next Michael Jordan and, as the stress of it caught up with him, he went into the worst slump of his career. Former basketball great Magic Johnson watched Bryant play and was alarmed enough to call him on the road to share his observation that Bryant was "not having fun anymore." Magic's advice to Bryant: "Go out and have a good time — and the greatness will come."

Whatever your method of dealing with stress, it's good to have an organized approach. Most of the ten leading causes of death are stress-related. Vascular diseases, cancer, cirrhosis, accidents all have a linkage with stress. Of course, the best course is to have a job where unhealthy stress is limited. Workplaces where there's lots of laughter normally indicate contentment. They are not only healthier but also conducive to employees' commitment, enthusiasm, creativity and productivity.

Adding humor, fun and play to the workplace will result in lowered absenteeism and a more enthusiastic, committed workforce willing to expend greater energy to increase productivity and generate more profits.

There are very few guarantees in life, but here is one: Whatever is not working well or whatever you would like to improve, try making it fun. It will improve. You'll get better at it if you're having fun doing it.

Chapter Six

Be a Better Leader

"One test of leadership is to turn around and see if anyone is following you."
—Anon.

The essence of leadership is helping people develop and deliver their full potential. It is more about being a coach than a quarterback, more of a rudder than a propeller. Like the leader of a championship sports team, creating winners involves selecting, training, leading and motivating people.

Some managers believe that using humor in relationships with subordinates will diminish their authority. Superior performance, however, is the result of commitment rather than authority. There is a subtle but important difference between management and leadership. This difference can be seen when examining why people do things. People act as a result of being compelled or impelled. While both are forces that cause people to act, the difference is in the reasons they do so, and therein we find the dichotomy between management and leadership.

Most leaders are followed because they are seen as confident, secure and mature. These qualities are all manifested by a sense of humor and the ability to

109

laugh at one's self. As discussed earlier, self-effacing humor is one of the characteristics of charisma. And charisma is an essential element of leadership. Vision, a prized managerial attribute, is the ability to see unexpected connections. A joke is the yoking of utterly disparate things. Thus, there is a connection between the two.

Injecting liberal doses of humor into the workplace is a departure from tradition. Over the past several years, what had previously been considered "Pollyannaism" is now being accepted and implemented in many forms. It is all part of creating a caring, sharing atmosphere full of mutual respect. It is the same attribute you'll find by peeking into the makeup of championship sports teams, crack combat units or other cohesive and well-functioning groups.

But humor, fun and play are not stand-alone elements in an organization that operates in a spirited environment. There are some other conditions that must be present. The organization must also have a sense of mission, an esprit de corps, open lines of communication and a tolerance of reasonable failure. And the employees must feel empowered.

Subordinating self-interests

Continental Airline's national ranking went from fourth from the bottom to second place, and from bankruptcy to a $640 million profit with one billion dollars in reserves. How? Management got all the employees working together and they made coming to work an enjoyable experience. The annals of business history are replete with such stories. Teamwork and job enjoyment are essential to business success. The only question seems to be, how are they best achieved?

Teamwork is the subjugation of the interests of the individual to those of the group. People are only willing to give up their own interests where there is a high level of trust and genuine affection for team members. Such situations are usually manifested by laughter, fun and play. When first-year coach Mike Schleelein joined the San Diego Chargers football team, he all but dared a handful of players to tape him up and douse him with Gatorade — a tradition with rookie coaches. Several linemen took up the challenge and did just that. The strength and conditioning coach took it good-naturedly. The prank was caught on videotape and shown during the rookie show that captures practical jokes and other antics used to welcome new players. The point is that strong teams have an egalitarian attitude among leaders and team members.

Bill Parcells, coach of several well-performing NFL teams, (NY Giants, New England Patriots, NY Jets) is known variously as "Charlie the Tuna" and the "Big Tuna." The New York Jets created a "Tuna award," which was not meant to be a compliment. One chilly autumn afternoon, University of Pittsburgh football coach Walt Harris walked onto the practice field and noticed some of his players were wearing spandex under their pads. Harris asked an equipment manager why. "It's cold, coach," the manager said. Harris turned his gaze on the manager and said, "I'll tell them when it's cold." Thereafter, Harris was dubbed "Walt the Weatherman." Teams react to leadership, whether it's positive or negative.

Selecting your team

It is most important to select members/employees who can perform well when the essential elements are provided. Hire people who are interested in having fun. This doesn't mean hiring someone who is predisposed to telling jokes all day or a person who yuk yuks all the time. It doesn't mean ignoring qualifications. It means selecting employees who are more inclined to think of their work as enjoyable and not take themselves too seriously.

This can be done by asking appropriate questions during the job interview. You might ask potential employees how they feel about "going to work to have fun." You might ask if they know the difference between being serious and being solemn. Or, come up with an unorthodox method of testing their creativity and propensity toward fun. One company gives job applicants a paper bag and tells them to do something creative with it.

Southwest Airlines, for example, is a company where hiring is seen as a religion. Their policy is to "hire for attitude and train for skills." They believe attitude is developed over the years, based on individual experiences. It is a fait accompli. It is what the applicant will bring to the job. And they believe that attitude is contagious and will spill over to the entire organization.

How do they assess attitude? They ask such questions as when was the last time the applicant used humor to defuse a situation? When was the last opportunity to break the rules? — or, as they put it — "color outside the lines."

They ask candidates to prepare a brief presentation about themselves. Then they observe how other job candidates are behaving during the presentation. They are most interested in those who are empathizing with the speaker, rather than those working on their own delivery.

They consider employee selection a top priority. On one occasion, in an effort to fill 5,473 jobs, they received 125,000 applications, interviewed 38,000 of those, and hired 5,444.

Setting the stage for learning

People learn pretty much the same as other animals. They respond to kindness in atmospheres of nonthreatening fun. Humor is important to training because it establishes the proper environment. People learn in relaxed, open atmospheres. Where there is tenseness, rigidity and a fear of failing, people do not learn. They slip into a "closed mode." This is a disposition wherein our defenses are up and we are afraid of looking foolish or stupid. It is not conducive to learning because we are too intent on defense to be *receptive*. People do not learn by having information forced into their brains. Knowledge has to be sucked in — rather than pushed in. This is best done by creating a mind-set thirsty for wisdom. Heightening interest in the subject matter is a key to creating that state of mind.

> *"Teaching is a performing art"*
>
> —Bob Ross

When it was discovered that children were terribly deficient in geography, a national project was initiated to teach the subject through games. It has been proven that making learning fun increases interest and attention and provides memory pegs.

The rules of communication and selling apply in training. Humor can be used to enhance your likability, thus building rapport and making your message more acceptable, enlarging attention, interest and increasing remembrance. General Motors has a film used to train employees in making the sale. It contains skits that show a salesman who talks too much, one who fails to close the deal even though the customer wants to buy, and depicts other situations in a humorous light to instill the points.

A little humor promotes camaraderie between teacher and student. It reduces the fear of failure which is crucial to the training process because permission to fail is permission to learn.

To establish an environment for training, build it around some humor, fun and play. These things automatically (assuming other obstacles are not present) move people into an open mode and engender feelings of acceptance and non-defensive behavior.

Conveying the message

Bill Nye, known as the "Science Guy" draws on his experience not just as a scientist, but as an entertainer as well. After graduating with an engineering degree from Cornell University, Nye worked part-time, after-hours as a stand-up comedian. He uses his background in both fields to teach his millions of television viewers about the wonders of science. In one case, he appeared on television wearing a lab coat and safety goggles and dunked an onion in liquid nitrogen. The onion shattered and the audience went wild, winning him a local Emmy award for the bit.

Making your point with humor and other theatrics makes them both palatable and memorable. Humor sugarcoats messages and facilitates their acceptability. And just as any memory course teaches you to make wild associations, your retention is dramatically increased if humor is used to anchor it. Humor refocuses attention and heightens interest. Laughing listeners learn more. Humor has been shown to enhance retention up to 800 percent! Studies show that this requires relevant humor. In other words, the humor must be tied to the subject matter. If your subject has you stumped, you can make humor relevant by the clever use of segues.

General Charles Krulak is a tough guy with a tough job. He is commandant of the Marine Corps. He stands only 5-foot-6 and did not graduate from high school. He regularly visits bases and has become famous for hanging out with his troops. While rank is a difficult gap to bridge, he breaks the ice and maintains his friendly image with humor. "Who's the shortest Marine here besides me?" he asks. When he finds a young man shorter than he is, he tells a photographer to "take a zillion pictures of me being taller." Then he gives the prized souvenir to the more diminutive comrade. The patriarch and leader of 174,000 Marines will ask a formation of his charges how many do not have a high school diploma. Then, he'll be the only one to raise his hand — making the point that Marines are better educated today. He builds himself up with his troops by putting himself down.

Motivation: making it fun!

In his first twelve seasons as manager of the Los Angeles Dodgers, Tommy Lasorda led his team to six division titles, four pennants and two World Series victories. Lasorda credits the inspiration for his managing style to a can of evaporated milk he spotted on his kitchen table when he was fifteen. It said, "Contented cows give better milk." As Lasorda himself put it: "I am of the belief that contented people give better performances. I try to make it fun for them."

When new coaches take over NFL teams, they are usually called upon to offer up their ideas about turning the team around. The most common remark heard is, "We're going to put some fun back into the game." Teams with losing seasons tend to tighten up. The stress of failure in this highly competitive sport is telling. Winning teams, on the other hand, tend to be having lots of fun. This is a self-fulfilling prophecy. Having fun fosters top performance.

Find ways to reward your team members with some humor, fun and play. The Tampa Bay Buccaneers football team, for example, applies the light touch by rewarding the special teams' player of the week. When the game film is reviewed, all the other players sit in regular institutional chairs while the player of the week sits in an over-stuffed living room chair.

Laughter is a mark of winning teams

The camaraderie that comes from having fun together is common to all winning teams. I remember reading about a kicker with the Detroit Lions named Benny Ricardo. His teammates would play tricks on him because he was a kicker. He got even with them by being more creative with his pranks. He would stretch Saran Wrap over the urinal to the point of invisibility and he'd put dark shoe polish on the black toilet seat. His favorite weapon was baby shampoo, highly concentrated, and poured into the hair of a showering teammate in mid-rinse. While his eyes were closed, the player couldn't see Ricardo slowly emptying the entire bottle on his head.

The Denver Broncos football team has a "kangaroo court" which fines coaches and players for such things as accepting praise, receiving the game ball and acting like a prima donna. The fines, which total between $10,000 and $20,000 a season, go into a fund for the offensive line to have a party at the end of the year.

Many sports teams find ways to incorporate humor, fun and play into their regimen. It relieves tension, lightens up the group and provides a spirit of cohesion. Virtually every major league baseball team has some method of injecting fun into the atmosphere. The Baltimore Orioles have an annual practical joke they play on their rookies. They pack away their suits and replace them with Salvation Army remnants. They travel to an away game wearing mismatched, loud, checks-and-plaids combinations along with weird looking shoes and socks.

"Leaders and tyrants are opposites."

—Anon.

The New Orleans Saints professional football team was not winning their share of games in the beginning of the 1996 season. So when they were about to play the equally odious Cardinals, they brought in Ava Kay Jones, also known as The High Priestess of Voodoo.

She showed up at the Superdome with a fifteen-foot voodoo doll dressed in Saints duds. The doll was strung up outside the main entrance and passersby were invited to tack notes onto it to encourage the team. Before kickoff the following day, it was put into a dumpster and taken to a secret burial site — to break the hex.

Employees of the Minneapolis ad agency Carmichael Lynch all have Kelly-green cardigans and get one arm stripe for each year of service. Ten-year vets get combat helmets. The company thrives on humor, fun and play. On "Dog Days" employees bring their pets to the office to perform tricks. They painted their building with different colored dots. Up close, the dots are meaningless. Viewed at a distance, they reveal the word "subliminal."

Breaking barriers

Essential to building a spirited environment and the free flow of information is a culture that condones failure in acceptable doses. Employees won't offer their ideas and techniques for improving the organization if they know they'll get beat up for failure. There are a number of characteristics that combine to constitute an organization's "corporate culture." Corporate culture is defined as the internal social climate of a business organization. It consists of the values, beliefs and attitudes of its employees, the leadership style of its management, and the way in which it conducts its business.

Working with so many different companies as I do, it is difficult not to notice the variance in corporate cultures. One telltale sign which reveals a great deal about an organization is what they celebrate. It's not unusual for organizations to celebrate success, but we find it interesting that some celebrate after a failure. But they aren't celebrating the fact that they failed. They are celebrating the effort that was put forth.

I was speaking with the CEO of a company that had just lost a major contract to a competitor. He explained that his celebration was to acknowledge his people's effort and the quality of their work. He wanted to reassure them that everything was okay; the effort was appreciated.

"Behold the turtle — he makes progress only when his neck is out."
—Anon.

Creativity means taking risks. Failure will inevitably result from people trying new ideas and techniques. So if this is desirable in an organization, it should be encouraged and even celebrated.

One executive, reasoning that a mistake is only a failure if you don't learn from it, startled his top staff by confessing a major mistake he had recently made and challenged them to top it for a cash reward. He subsequently introduced a program that offered $250 every month for the greatest mistake. This encouraged management to acknowledge their errors and share the information. He calculated that $250 divided by his 20 top staff members equaled only $12.50 — a cheap way to learn and grow.

There is a well-known story about Thomas Watson, Sr., the legendary head of IBM. A young executive made a $10 million dollar mistake and was called into Mr. Watson's office. As he approached the CEO, he said, "I guess you're going to fire me." Watson responded, "Fire you? Heavens no! We've just invested $10 million dollars in your education!"

Healthy environments do not punish employees for making mistakes. People who stand still may avoid stubbing their toes, but they won't make much progress. Trying new ideas is sure to result in mistakes. Failure should be our teacher, not our undertaker. Success is, after all, a positive manipulation of failure.

Humor can be used effectively in virtually all aspects of the workplace. Of course, the ripest and most advantageous activity lending itself to humor is the meeting. This has been almost unanimously identified as the most wasted time

116

of any business activity. Large parts of the day are dedicated to these meetings where employees sit, fighting for consciousness, while colleagues describe projects that have nothing to do with them.

The biggest waste of organizational time

Meetings are supposed to be held to exchange information and solve problems. Such activities require receptivity, candor and creativity. None of those things happen in formal, structured, closed-mode environments. People are simply not open, sharing, candid and creative in that kind of atmosphere.

Look for ways to instill humor, fun and play into these sessions. Borrow from President John F. Kennedy and begin your meetings with everybody stating, "I'm healthy, I'm happy, I'm here for fun." Then begin your meeting with a joke. Have the "joke master" be a revolving assignment with a different person providing a joke each time. Use cartoons in your handouts. Euphemize the minutes. Have some humorous awards. If someone shows up late, require them to offer a creative but absolutely ridiculous excuse for their tardiness. Name your meeting room after some antagonist or other unlikely person. If your company reported a big profit, find a way to use that to add some fun. If you're experiencing some adversity, play off of that. Executive Editor Jerry Ceppos presided over a staff meeting at the San Jose *Mercury News* wearing a camouflaged army helmet. He was poking fun at the foxhole he finds himself and the big guns of the rival media trained at him.

Reports, such as annual reports, are fertile ground for the use of humor. Here's an example of humor used in this way from ASK Computer Systems Inc.:

"One of America's greatest management philosophers once said, 'If you don't know where you're going you might end up somewhere else.' Casey Stengel may have mangled the language, but he didn't mince words. He understood the importance of strategy and planning in the achievement of ultimate goals. And ASK agrees with his philosophy — that's why the company has a comprehensive strategy to maintain its leadership position into the next decade and beyond."

Bringing it all together

It was halftime and Notre Dame was losing badly. The Fighting Irish knew they were due for a fiery pep talk from their coach, Knute Rockne. After all, he was known for his motivational speeches that had taken previous teams to unprecedented fame. But halftone was almost over and, mysteriously, he never came! Then, just as the team prepared to take the field for the final period,

Rockne stuck his head in the locker room door and said, "Oh, pardon me. I was looking for the Notre Dame football team." He turned and left. The team went back onto the field and trounced their opponents. Rockne's appearance combined good showmanship with good management. Motivation almost always comes from within. People do things for one of three reasons; they are being threatened, bribed or cajoled. Rockne cajoled his team using some imagination and showmanship.

Modern managers usually don't think of themselves as being in show business. Yet they often use the techniques of the profession to excel in their jobs. Drawing on elements of the theater to get their points across and move their "audiences," astute managers are tapping some show business concepts to open up meetings — and increase production.

IBM, known for its quality customer service, literally sets the stage to encourage service excellence. Often corporate meetings are interrupted by a person pushing a wheelbarrow full of cash. The cash is then presented to an employee, and the audience is told what the person did to promote service excellence. Talk about a "show stopper!"

"Authority makes some people grow — others just swell"

— Anon.

If you'd like to make your own debut, a good place to start is your next organizational meeting. It's an ideal setting to use your show business instincts to inject some humor, fun and play. If you're not funny, don't worry about it; take your turn and assign the job on a revolving basis to other "cast" members. Remember, you're the director/producer. The humorous scripting of an awards ceremony like the Oscars or Emmys is well within the range of almost any company. Begin with a relevant joke. Corporate humor books are full of generic examples. Simply tailor the joke to your group. Remember, humor increases message retention by up to 800 percent. Little wonder that two of every three major advertising messages employ an amusing theme.

You might ask yourself what talent you have that can be entertaining and useful. One company CEO found his skills at ventriloquism valuable. He uses a dummy to communicate certain information at staff meetings. The dummy has become such an integral part of this organization that it's considered a member of the upper management team. In fact, if you visit this company's offices, you'll find the dummy's picture, along with portraits of the agency's founders, hanging in the waiting room.

You don't have to throw your voice or do a song and dance act to give your organization a taste of showbiz. Announcing new policies or procedures would seem to be a rather simple process. But is anybody listening? Many a manager or CEO has found that these proclamations go unheard. More progressive managers use a little showbiz as a method of gaining attention. A Silicon Valley firm, for example, closed their 2,000-worker plant for a day and threw a giant barbecue in the parking lot to launch its new program. Getting the attention of the audience is one of the first rules of show business.

Windy speakers and nodding heads

Another lesson from showbiz is to leave your audience wanting more. How many people in your organization want more meetings? If the answer is a big laugh and a resounding cry for fewer meetings, you may want to look again to show business for some ideas. That's exactly what Teradyne, a Boston-based company, did. After several years of holding quarterly meetings with pie charts and overhead slide projectors to try to improve productivity and customer satisfaction, the $400 million company found it was producing only windy speakers and nodding heads — no results. Employees found the meetings boring. They dreaded them. So management enlisted the aid of employees to make the process work. Meetings were never the same.

Employees were given a free hand to produce these "Zero Defects Day" meetings, with the proviso that they stay within budget. The committee made its showbiz debut with a spoof of the television game show "Wheel of Fortune." It featured a manager in the role of host Pat Sajak and another (bearded) employee wearing a wig and evening gown playing the part of "Vanna." The show was an instant hit. After the usual presentation of measurements and awards, the curtain was raised and the show began. Each committee member had a role, from announcer to cameraman to producer. Employees gave the meeting rave reviews. Comments ranged from, "Oh no, not another ZD Day" to "I wonder what they're going to do next quarter."

Now you might ask, "What's effective about a couple of guys impersonating game show stars?" The meeting was a success in stirring up fun, promoting employee enthusiasm and spotlighting employees' hidden talents. Clearly, entertainment put across their message about quality. What followed were more parodies of television programs. They staged a mock talk show, and to stress the cost of mistakes in manufacturing, produced a game show called, "The Cost Is Right," where contestants guessed the cost of specific defects in their manufacturing process. That was followed by "Foundry Feud," with employees competing to answer questions about quality awareness.

Management found that the show business approach was communicating messages about quality that would have fallen flat in the old style meetings.

What was the payoff? After five years, late delivery was reduced by 40 percent, returns from one division were reduced by 85 percent, defects in one area were cut by 77 percent, and delayed shipping had fallen by 85 percent.

In today's world, effective management demands getting the best from your team — just as Knute Rockne did. And to do that, you'll do well to borrow from show business. If you were going to put together an award-winning Broadway production, you'd start with a great cast (employees) and good direction (training, motivation) .

As managers scramble to find ways to select, motivate and inspire their work teams, nothing is out of bounds. If you're looking for excellence, it might be well to remember that leadership is about molding moods. And that's also the essence of show business. Break a leg!

"The health of any organization is directly proportionate
to its ability to laugh at itself."

—Bob Basso

Chapter Seven

Defuse Hostility & Turn Confrontation into Cooperation

"Humor can be an incredible, lacerating and effective weapon."
—Carl Hiaasen

The story is told of Elmer Kelen, a man who had hired a young Hungarian artist by the name of Arpad Sebesy to do his portrait. When Kelen arrived to pick up the painting he immediately informed the artist that it didn't resemble him. He refused to take possession and he refused to pay the previously agreed upon price of five hundred pengos. The artist was dismayed but kept his wits about him. "Will you give me a letter saying you refused the portrait because it doesn't look like you," he asked. Happy to get off the hook, Kelen complied.

A few months later there was an exhibition at the Gallery of Fine Arts in Budapest. Following its opening, Kelen's phone began to ring. He soon appeared at the gallery and went to the section where a Sebesy painting was on display. It was the very portrait he had rejected. He glanced at the title and stormed off to the office of the gallery director demanding that the painting be removed at once. The director explained that all paintings were under contract for a six-month period. "But it will make me the laughing stock of Budapest," yelled Kelen. "It's libelous. I'll sue!"

"Just a moment," said the director. He pulled from his desk the letter Kelen had written at Sebesy's request. Showing him the letter, he said, "You, yourself, acknowledged that the painting does not resemble you."

In desperation, Kelen offered to buy the painting only to find the price had gone up tenfold. But he wrote out the check and bought it — for five thousand pengos.

Sebesy had not only gotten ten times his original price but took sweet revenge too, simply by titling the painting *Portrait of a Thief.*

Go with the flow

When we are very small we are taught to resist. When another student at school pushes us, we are told to "push him back." Yet if he is stronger, a pushing contest will favor him. Skillfully giving way is a better tactic because it turns the aggressive force of the attacker against himself. In Judo, students learn the story of the supple reed and the mighty oak tree. In a violent storm, the mighty oak will be toppled, but the flexible reed will bend in the wind, and by giving way to this superior force, will survive. Judo, translated, means "gentle way."

Thus, in Judo and Aikido, you don't resist force, you go with the flow! This same principle can be used very effectively in verbal confrontation by employing humor. Using this principle means not reacting in a way that could be construed as resistance. It means redirecting the verbal attack to work against the attacker.

When John Tesh, popular musician and former host of the television program *Entertainment Tonight,* showed up in Detroit, he was met by a group of detractors. The National Anti-Tesh Action Society picketed him. Tesh, apparently in appreciation of the fact that he had his own protest group, wanted his picture taken with the pickets. But when he showed up for the photo, they took off. Is there a lesson here? By "joining" the group, he frustrated their efforts. Similarly, I have often read about movie stars and other celebrities getting into fist fights and other rows with the paparazzi who haunt them. I always wonder what would happen if instead they struck a professional pose for about five minutes. My guess is that the tabloid photographers would take off.

A recent example of going with the flow occurred when Senator John Burton of the California legislature became frustrated with what he believed was Governor Pete Wilson's philosophy that people are poor because they want to be poor. The liberal democrat introduced legislation that would make it a crime to be poor and to establish a state orphan asylum to house the children of poor people. Taking something to its illogically-humorous extreme is an effective way to demonstrate its ludicrous nature.

This technique was used in San Francisco by opponents of a local bond issue to raise money for a new football stadium. The group adopted the name "Multimillionaires For Corporate Welfare" and then ostensibly *backed* the bond issue. As such, they submitted the ballot argument *for* the stadium bonds. The merry pranksters offered the argument that the DeBartolos (team owners and multi-millionaires) need the public money because they live in Ohio and must maintain two residences. The Registrar of Voters ultimately switched the argument from the support side to the opposition section of the pamphlet but the lampoon effectively made their point against the proposal.

A similar technique was used by San Diegan Josh Baxt in a local effort to obtain public financing for a new library. The city was embroiled in a controversial effort to build a new football stadium. In the midst of this came a proposal for a new library. Signs began appearing around town that read, "Build stadiems, not libraries." The misspelled signs were the subject of several news articles due to their humorous but obviously inherent point. Finally, Josh "fessed up" and admitted the hoax; acknowledging that he was pro-library rather than pro-stadium. Again, the humor solution accomplished its purpose better than any more direct approach could have.

Hillary and Eleanor

First lady Hillary Clinton had some White House sessions with new-age psychic researcher Jean Houston. One of the exercises was to engage in an imaginary conversation with someone whom Mrs. Clinton admired. She chose Eleanor Roosevelt. But when the press found out about it, there was a lot of publicity and much of it put a wacky spin on the story. So, when the first lady showed up at a Nashville conference a couple of days later, she defused the issue by joking that she had just had an imaginary talk with Eleanor Roosevelt — "and she thinks this (the appearance) is a terrific idea." The audience laughed appreciably and the experience became a non-issue.

The winter of 1998 was particularly harsh because of a condition known as "El Nino." It took its toll throughout the country but was especially troublesome in California. In the midst of this we find Alfonso Nino, who was listed in a California phone book as "Al Nino." It's hard to believe, but he would regularly get calls from people who would confuse him with the weather phenomenon El Nino. They would call and say something like "Why are you doing this?" Rather than fight the issue, he'd say "I thought maybe it would be kind of fun." Do you think Al has a sense of humor?

Sometimes humor can be used as a mirror to show people how silly they are behaving or to reflect discontent over a situation. Rather than throwing back your head and guffawing at the stupidity of others, it is much more effective to use humor to create a mirror similar to fun-house mirrors in an amusement park. You can make your point without meanness or ridicule by illuminating the path to enlightenment through humor.

When the top executives of seven major airlines testified before a Senate committee on antitrust issues, they were crammed together at the witness table. Senator Mike DeWine of Ohio quipped, "Sorry about the crowding, but welcome to coach class."

"Anyone without a sense of humor is at the mercy of everyone else."
—William Rotsler

The perfect squelch

I have a friend who is a comedian. While traveling on a certain airline he found the coffee very disappointing and wrote the CEO a letter of complaint, informing him that he was telling his audiences about the terrible coffee being served. The CEO responded by writing that he had caught my friend's act and hadn't been going around telling people how awful *it* was. But, so as not to be flippant (very important in using humor this way) he followed his rejoinder with an acknowledgment of the deficient coffee and his promise to look into the matter with an eye toward improvement.

Former congressman Bob Dornan is an ultraconservative Republican (known as B-1 Bob) who made a career of bashing liberals, feminists, gays and communists. He was full of invective and seemed to detest President Clinton. He would denounce the president as a "womanizer," an "adulterer" and a "disgraced draft dodger" who "demeans the office with his silk girlie-girlie jogging pants showing those beautiful white doughboy thighs of his."

And those were the *complimentary* things he said about the president. No, just kidding. But how could the president respond without dignifying those remarks and, at the same time, still seem presidential? When the press asked the president about Dornan's remarks, here was Clinton's response: "Every time I see Dornan, he looks like he needs a rabies shot."

The president did not try to refute the charges. But instead of making remarks about Dornan's physical appearance, he merely commented on his pit-bull viciousness. Using the humor solution in his reply he was able to be both effective and presidential.

History has recorded many examples of the clever retort. One of the wittiest is attributed to 18th century British politician John Wilkes. Lord Sandwich, his antagonist, suggested that Wilkes would die either of the pox or the gallows. Wilkes responded, "that will depend on whether I embrace your lordship's mistress or your lordship's principles."

Winston Churchill was considered a grand master of the perfect squelch. Irish playwright Bernard Shaw once invited him to the opening-night of one of his plays. Shaw sent him two tickets with a note explaining that one of them was "for a friend — if you have one." Churchill wrote back that he would be unable to attend but asked if he could have tickets for the second-night performance —"if there is one."

"The softest things in the world overcome the hardest things in the world."
—Lao-tzu

In 1913, when New York performers tried to organize the Actors' Equity Association, they found a formidable opponent in George M. Cohan, who at the time was arguably the greatest star and producer on Broadway. The original Yankee Doodle Dandy threatened to shut out the union from his productions and, to publicize his opposition, he purchased large ads in the New York newspapers with the following notice: "I'd sooner lose every dollar I have and make my living as an elevator operator than do business with Actors' Equity." The next day the union hung out a sign that read: "Wanted — elevator operator. George M. Cohan preferred."

Al Hirschfeld, a well-known caricaturist of Broadway and film stars, did a drawing of Broadway producer David Merrick — admittedly not one of his favorite characters. It featured Merrick as a snaggle-toothed Santa Claus. Hirschfeld acknowledged he'd done it as viciously as he could. Merrick bought the drawing and used it as a Christmas card, leaving the cartoonist wondering what he'd done wrong.

Amusing tactics

When someone attacks you, whether it is by impugning your character, criticizing, accusing or generally defaming you, you have options similar to being physically attacked. You can deflect it, you can counterpunch, or you can use the principal of Judo and redirect the advancing force.

When the Winston-Salem, North Carolina, Board of Aldermen announced they were considering a forty-one percent hike in property assessment, local prankster Joseph King went to work. He sponsored a latter-day Lady Godiva who rode through town in the (almost) altogether. It may not have thwarted enactment of the tax increase but calling attention to a perceived negative event with humorous theatrics certainly assured maximum publicity and public awareness.

Attacking the vulnerable point

Famous hoaxer, Alan Abel, got into a tiff with a large insurance company that had insured a loss he incurred. They offered him substantially less than what he felt he was due. When he objected they gave him an ultimatum: "Take what we're offering or sue us!" Abel said he would do neither! The next morning, outside the insurance giant's headquarters Abel appeared, parading back and forth with a large sign that read: "Why is Interstate Insurance (not its real name) failing?" And in small letters below that was a barely legible postscript: "to treat their customers fairly."

People on their way to work saw the sign and began calling the insurance company to inquire about their financial condition and, in some cases, to cancel their policies. It wasn't long before a company executive was on the sidewalk with a check for the full amount claimed by Abel. The master of the humor solution realized he had a third alternative that most of us would not have recognized. Using his wit and finding a vulnerable point to attack, he found a way that was faster, less expensive and more effective than litigation. The humor solution at its finest!

When a San Diego barber was told by the city that he could not erect a roadside sign directing people to his hair salon, he dressed up as a barber pole and paraded around during rush hour. Opposition can be demonstrated in socially acceptable ways when expressed humorously.

The humorous award

One way to get at people who annoy you is to create an "award." This is a method akin to the Judo approach in that you are "spotlighting, endorsing and applauding" the action with tongue in cheek in order to lampoon it.

Senator William Proxmire has long had his "Golden Fleece Award." It has enabled him to publicly identify people and organizations he feels are unjustly enriching themselves at the public's expense. Having an award that is ongoing adds credibility to the award and enhances its publicity value. Awards tend to gather prestige commensurate with their longevity.

The Center for Science in the Public Interest established the Harlan Page Hubbard awards, named after a pioneer advertiser of patent medicines that were supposed to cure whatever ailed you. This was a mock award to counter the advertising industry's coveted "Clio" awards. They were given for the year's most misleading, unfair or irresponsible ad campaign. Winners were given (if they chose to accept them) a bronze-colored victory figure grasping a lemon. A couple of 1989 annual winners: The U.S. Council for Energy Awareness (a previous Hubbard recipient) was singled out for "claiming that nuclear power can reduce oil imports when, in fact, most oil is used for gasoline for which nuclear power cannot substitute."

TWA was also "honored" for advertising a $298 round-trip fare to London including hotel and car "when the actual cost of the trip ranges from more than $700 to $1400," according to the CSPI.

Their "rediscovery of the wheel award" went to a $4.4 million project of continuing studies on "wood utilization." The authors predicted that by the time the research ends in 1997, perhaps the toothpick will have been discovered.

Senator Thad Cochran, (R.-Miss.) won the "Dr. Dolittle weird science award" for adding $200,000 to an appropriations bill for "entomology acoustics detection" to find noisy insects in his home state.

Awards are an excellent and socially acceptable way of opposing and calling attention to activity deserving of ridicule. Citizens Against Lawsuit Abuse (CALA) opposes what they consider to be frivolous law suits. They promote their cause by giving out the "Loony Lawsuit Award." This award generates publicity by pressing satire into service. Its humorous and offbeat nature attracts news articles calling attention to these legal excesses. The 1996 award went to a woman who claimed damages from a K-mart store after she pulled out the bottom box at a blender display and brought the stack down on her. A previous winner in the game of tort sport was a Grateful Dead fan who sued his law partner for making fun of Jerry Garcia's (former band member) death.

Tort sport

Back in 1970, Grove Press, Inc. received a letter from Coca Cola protesting an advertisement in the *New York Times* for *Diary of a Harlem Schoolteacher* by Jim Haskins. The theme of the ad was "This book is like a weapon . . . it's the real thing."

Pointing out that Coca Cola had made use of "It's the Real Thing" to advertise their product prior to the publication of the book, it requested a discontinuance of use of the theme in connection with the book. In support of their position, they cited the "likelihood of confusion as to the source or sponsorship of the goods."

The publisher's reply reverted to humor to make their point. Expressing sympathy for their feeling of a proprietary interest in the slogan, the writer said he understood how the public might be confused by use of the slogan and "mistake a book by a Harlem schoolteacher for a six-pack of Cola Cola." Thus, they promised to request all sales personnel to make sure that what the customer wanted was a book, rather than a Coke.

Rather than openly contest Coca Cola's position, they simply acquiesced, acknowledging their proprietary rights and offering a practical, if tongue-in-cheek, solution.

Repartee

When engaging in verbal combat one should consider whether it will be for the benefit of the other party or for public consumption. Each calls for a different strategy.

When Bob Dole faced his own series of debates in 1996, he knew that humor would serve him well. But how to use it? *Newsweek* magazine suggested a line for him such as, "I knew Tom Jefferson. You're not Jefferson." Such humor would be especially appropriate and effective since the former senator was considered relatively old and had a reputation for being stodgy and grumpy. James Carville, advisor to President Clinton, suggested that the first thing out of Bob Dole's mouth should be a joke. Since Dole vetoed the idea of including Ross Perot in the debates, he could use some self-deprecating humor involving Mr. Perot. Carville suggests looking at his watch, glancing around the room (makes the humor go over twice as well) and saying, "Hey, anybody know what happened to Ross? Should we give him a few more minutes, or start now?" As Carville said, it would bring the whole place down and score points for good humor.

A few years ago I was in Seattle during the political season. I remember reading in the local newspaper about two men running for congress. One had accused the other of coloring his hair. He said he knew he colored it because he could see a telltale sign from his television appearances. What was interesting to me was that the fellow making the claim was bald. Now I don't know what this had to do with their congressional race or how this public argument turned out, but I recall thinking that the one who wins this follicle-based argument will be the one who knows how to best the other with humor. To me, the solution was clearly in a topping (no pun intended) humorous remark.

Former U.S. Senator Stephen Young of Ohio used to deal with crank letters by returning them to the sender with a note attached that read: "This letter came across my desk several days ago. I'm sending it to you in the belief that as a responsible citizen you would want to know there is some idiot out there sending out this kind of nonsense over your signature."

When a reader wrote to columnist Mike Royko, at the *Chicago Tribune*, it was an insulting missive. The detractor said he understood Mr. Royko had been writing his column for about twenty-five years and he didn't see how anybody as stupid as Royko could do it that long. Royko responded that the writer had spotted the secret to his longevity (stupidity). "By the way," he added, "you might buy yourself a typewriter and give it a try. Your letter shows considerable promise."

A protest is always more effective if it is staged with some theater. When the San Diego Animal Advocates planned to protest their local zoo's practice of selling animals to game ranches, they staged some Christmas caroling at the zoo's main gate during the holiday season. But their song list included "Oh Come All Ye Hunters," and "God Rest Ye Helpless Animals."

The Reverend Henry Ward Beecher came into his church one morning and found a letter addressed to him which contained a single word: "Fool." He told the congregation about it and added, "I have known many an instance of a man writing a letter and forgetting to sign his name, but this is the only instance I have ever known of a man signing his name and forgetting to write the letter."

The humor boomerang

Another tactic is to reframe the charge or insult in such a way as to send it back to the person or use it in another context to make it an asset. A classic case of turning the tables occurred during the ongoing battle between ultra-conservative U.S. Senator Jesse Helms and the homosexual community. In a fifteen-second video promoting San Francisco's Lesbian-Gay Freedom Day Parade, the committee used a clip of the North Carolina Republican. It seems that while arguing against the Senate confirmation of lesbian Roberta Achtenberg (as Assistant Secretary of HUD) Helms said, "That gay pride parade. . . I wish every American could have seen it." By taking a fifteen-second sound bite and using it in this style, the parade committee got a tongue-in-cheek endorsement and seized a promotional opportunity. It was really not dishonest because anyone who could recognize Senator Helms would have to know the comment was taken out of context and being used in a humorous fashion.

Peter Falk, star of the long-running series *Columbo*, has a glass eye. He explains that when he was young it bothered him and he would worry about people noticing it. But soon he rose above it by making jokes. Once in a high school baseball game, he slid into third base and the umpire called him out. He got angry and whipped out his glass eye and handed it to the umpire with the comment, "Here — you might see better with this one!"

Humor with a little shock value.

The next time you find yourself in a confrontational situation, stop, think and draw on your sense of humor to deal with it. I recall a situation in which I had hired a small contractor to install air conditioning in a hair salon my wife and I owned. He continually failed to perform the work even though I had advanced him some money. Finally, after exhausting polite requests to do the work, I sat down to think funny and came up with the solution. I knew the contractor was unschooled in legal matters and feared litigation.

I got some legal paper and wrote several long paragraphs about the situation, using legal mumbo jumbo. Sprinkled with lots of "party of the first part" and "party of the second part" I recounted the scenario and stated my intention to pursue the matter in court, utilizing lots of Latin words such as "prima facie." I'm quite sure the words — as intended — made little sense to the contractor. What influenced him was the legal jargon which he didn't understand but feared. He got the paper, looked it over and quickly performed.

Expounding on the absurdity

Turning the tables can take the form of an innocuous ploy or can be a more complex or laborious undertaking. Norman Cousins, in his book *Healing Heart*, relates a conflict he had some years ago with a telephone operator. After losing a dime to the coin-operated phone, he got a live operator and explained his plight. She told him the phone company would be happy to send him a refund if he would provide his name and address. Then he told her he thought it was absurd that they would spend postage and time instead of just putting his call through.

While he was expounding on this absurdity, he absently pressed the coin return lever and all the coins began to tumble out of the machine. He promptly told the operator what was occurring. She asked him if he would put the money back in the box. "Operator," he said, "if you will give me your name and address, I'll be happy to mail it to you."

Another such case of turning the tables involves the use of some esoteric law. In her book, *Loony Laws and Silly Statutes* (Sterling Publishing), author Sheryl Lindsell-Roberts tells the story of a traveler turned away from a posh Boston hotel because he was improperly attired. The man departed, put on immaculate clothes, then gathered up sheep, cattle and other animals and led them into the hotel lobby. The horrified clerk had little choice but to hand over a key because Boston law stipulated that a hotel or inn must make rooms available to a man and his livestock. This story got me to thinking about how these screwy laws could be used in humorously creative ways. She mentions, for example, that Connecticut law requires restaurants to offer nose-blowing and non-nose-blowing sections. I can't wait to be in that state and be denied a table in a restaurant there. I will consider conducting a citizen's arrest on the hostess for not meeting requirements of state law related to nose-blowing sections.

Using humor to diffuse hostility

Frederick Kappel, former chairman & CEO of AT&T was conducting the annual shareholder meeting. By the fourth hour, the affair had turned volatile. After a long, hectic session wherein Kappel had fielded many tough questions, a woman rose to announce she was unhappy over the large amount being donated to charity. How much, she asked him, was donated to charity? Replied Kappel, "Ten million dollars last year." The woman mockingly responded, "I think I'm going to faint." Said Kappel, "That would be very helpful." The audience laughed and applauded and the CEO was back in control.

There are several dynamics at work here. First, in confrontational situations it pays to "think funny" because that in itself relaxes you — which in turn helps you to think more clearly and thus to take and maintain control.

Second, the less threatening you are, the more the other person will relax — diminishing the tenseness that exacerbates these circumstances. If you can get the other person to laugh or even smile, you will gain their trust and approval.

Laughter normally puts us in the open mode where we leave our defensive posture and become less likely to give in to feelings of aggression. Research has shown that people cannot simultaneously entertain incompatible feelings such as anger and amusement. Thus, it is impossible to harbor ill feelings while you're laughing.

In using humor to diminish hostility, there are a couple of important points to consider. First, a distinction must be made between anger and hostility. They are often viewed as similar, but in fact they are quite different. Anger is an emotion while hostility reflects intention. While one is usually hostile when angry, the reverse is not necessarily true.

Second, for humor to work against hostility or anger, it must be considered funny by the recipient. In other words, it must "amuse" to "defuse." Therefore, it is critical to avoid the flippant retort or response. So if you're faced with anger, you must first diminish that emotion. Centering, or acknowledging the other person's position, is the best way to do this. "Well, Sam, I certainly can understand why you would feel that way." The idea here is to begin where they are. By sending them the message, "I got it!" you recognize their grievance — without necessarily agreeing with them. This does more than anything to bring them to a state of calmness, which is where they must be to deal with the hostility.

The dynamics of hostility

When we recognize hostile intentions, we automatically become threatened and move into the closed mode. It is quite natural, and indeed even functional, to retreat to our defensive mechanisms when threatened. Humor, if it is to move us from the closed to the open mode, must be relaxing and relieve the threat — at least temporarily. It can sometimes work if it is directed at the situation, but has better results if focused on the on the person initiating the humor.

Roger Ailes used to tell the story about the corporate executive who wanted to buy a large manufacturing firm. He and his attorney were invited to an "exploratory" meeting where they were met by the firm's CEO and an entire "roomful" of lawyers. He smiled and said, "Well, it looks like Butch & Sundance have just met the Bolivian Army." Everyone laughed. By breaking the ice with humor, the potentially hostile takeover was turned into a friendly merger. In this case the humor was focused on the "situation" and worked to defuse the hostility.

I remember reading some time back about a fellow whose firm bought out a shirt company. Employees were understandably apprehensive about their jobs and future. When he met with his new workers, the room was full of tension. The new owner began by discussing why he wanted to own the clothier. He praised the shirts made by these people in detail— the collars, the sleeves, cuffs. But, he said, there was one aspect of their shirts he was hoping to improve. At that point, he took off his suit jacket to reveal a totally shredded shirt. The employees laughed heartily and the tension diminished.

Diminishing hostility and tension

I recall a situation during my years in designing and implementing urban revitalization programs in various cities. We were redeveloping a large area of downtown Lansing, Michigan. We needed the power of eminent domain to proceed and there was substantial opposition to that aspect of the plan. The chairman of my board of directors, a local attorney and very witty guy, accompanied me to a raucous meeting of community members. In the midst of a heated discussion about eminent domain, Jack rose to spontaneously address the community group. He made only one brief statement, but it cracked up the audience and diminished the hostility and tension. He said: "Please keep in mind that eminent domain is not imminent."

Andre Tippett is Director of Player Resources for the New England Patriots professional football team and a former defensive player. He tells of the difficulties of sacking Denver Broncos quarterback John Elway. "Just when you think you have him lined up, he senses your presence and gives you a head and shoulder fake, leaving you in the dust." On one such occasion, Elway left Tippett grasping for air while he threw the ball upfield for a completion. Then, relates Tippett, Elway turned around and smiled at him and said, "Not bad speed for a white boy, huh?" Said Tippett, "I had wanted to hit him so bad. But, after he said that, all I could do was laugh." This is a good example of the impossibility of being angry and amused at the same time.

Another example involving professional sports was the case of basketball player Robert Horry of the Phoenix Suns. He became incensed after being taken out of a game by coach Danny Ainge and, on national television, threw a towel in the coach's face. Later, he called a press conference to apologize. If there was any doubt that the hostility between the two had dissipated, it was removed when, during the televised apology, coach Ainge walked by and threw a towel in Horry's face — and the player broke out in laughter.

Another way to observe the principle of giving way, as in Aikido, is to try this experiment. The next time you're in a mild argument with, say your spouse, and he or she says, "You're wrong!," say, "You're right. I'm wrong." Now what do they say? "You're right; I'm right, you're wrong!"

Suppose you are approached by a customer, your boss or anyone who is upset about your having forgotten something. Poking a little fun at yourself over the matter should bring them around. You can use humor to do this — perhaps saying something such as, "Darn it, if I get anymore forgetful they'll let me hide my own Easter eggs!" Since the humor is self-directed, it is an indirect method of apologizing and helps diminish the offense.

As stated before, my definition of having a sense of humor is being able to think funny and to laugh at yourself. Dealing effectively with hostility in the fashion explained here requires calling upon both of these skills. If you can do that, you'll be seen as incredibly charming, since it is a art form not known or practiced by many people.

Smoothing out the bumps

Whenever you are dealing with people, you must first open them up. As Golda Meir, former prime minister of Israel, used to say, "You can't shake hands with a clenched fist." Humor opens people up and breaks down resistance. That's why it can be used to deflect and defuse hostility, turning situations from combatible to compatible. When we openly and honestly show ourselves to others through self-effacing humor, we influence them to share their motives, dreams and goals.

Awkward business situations can be smoothed out with humor. AT&T grappled with how to structure an apology for committing a typographical error in its earnings report. Here's an apology based on the humor solution that they came up with (from *Focus*, an AT&T employee magazine): "Our February 9 issue reported our 1987 earnings per share as $1.88 billion. The addition of "billion" was a typesetter's error, and we apologize for any ecstasy the error may have caused." And when Delta Airlines changed gates for a departing flight several times, finally using the gate originally planned, it resulted in passengers running back and forth from gate to gate. They concluded the series of announcements with, "Thank you for participating in Delta's fitness program."

Disagree without being disagreeable

Humor can also be used during confrontations to "bring people around." This is tricky since it involves creating perspective in the mind of your antagonist.

I recall the case where an irate airline passenger was hassling an employee of the airline who was trying to straighten out the lost baggage situation. Finally the employee said, "Listen, there are only two people in the whole world that care about this situation, and one of them is rapidly losing interest."

A fellow told me about his type A behavior on the highway. It seems he drove with a lot of anxiety; annoyed with drivers who got in his way. One day, while his granddaughter was in the car with him, she observed his behavior and commented innocently, "What's the matter grandpa, are these people driving on your road?" The child's innocent humor allowed him to see the point of his obsessive behavior.

You can even make your criticism more palatable by framing it in a humorous context. When Mike Royko wrote about Jesse Jackson's verbosity he stated, "He lives to talk. He looks at a defenseless ear the way William "Refrigerator" Perry eyes a roast chicken." Can you see how humor takes some of the acidity out of your sour grapes?

Here are a few descriptive evaluations of different cheeses. While they are all critical, note the use of good-natured, humorous language:

"dry and mealy; tastes like a mouse pad,"

"tastes like Alpine socks after a day on the slopes,"

"tastes like an eraser I chewed on as a kid"

"flavor is like a Dr. Scholl's foot insert."

The film critic makes his point in an entertaining way. And speaking of cheese, here are a couple of movie critiques utilizing a humorous twist:

"The movie is one big piece of Swiss cheese, minus the cheese."

"Several of the characters are psychic, which puts them in the unique position of being able to understand what goes on in the movie."

When Nevada lawmakers decided to conduct a "fact-finding" mission by touring one of the state's legalized brothels, Jeff Ackerman, a newspaper editor, thought it was preposterous. But instead of writing a column railing against the idea, he offered this comment: "Except for the degree of pleasure they provide, lawmakers and prostitutes might actually have a lot in common." The legislators canceled the trip.

Rebuttals

There may be times in your life when you'll want to express your disappointment, disagreement, opposition or even your anger in an acceptable way. Other occasions may arise where you'll be attacked verbally by someone and feel a need to respond in some fashion. Humor will serve you well in all of these situations.

A salesman I know had expensed a new hat on his company account. The comptroller kept sending him notes stating that it would not be permitted. The salesman would respond each time by sending a note explaining how he had lost the hat he had replaced in a business-related predicament. Finally, after several of these exchanges, the salesman sent in his expenses with a note: "The hat is in here. See if you can find it."

From time to time you will encounter criticism or suffer insults. If you are in public life or if your job or avocation involves controversy, this will happen not infrequently. When it does occur you have a few choices. You can choose to ignore whatever verbal barb has been sent your way, and that may be most appropriate. But more often some sort of response will be required or expected. Unless an apology is in order, you basically have two options. You can refute the opposition, criticism or insult with facts and figures or you can use humor to deflect, rebut or diminish the insult or criticism.

Whether you are offering your own disagreement, disappointment or opposition or reacting to another's remarks, you can make your comments more effective and increase their acceptability by couching them in humor.

Politicians often use grainy, unflattering photographs of their political opponents in their advertisements and commercials. In the 1996 Republican primary, Malcomb Forbes kept running terribly uncomplimentary photos of opponent Bob Dole. During their primary debates, Dole confronted Forbes with this and offered him a photograph to use. It included Dole and his wife with their dog. The senator presented it to Forbes on national television, pointing out which was the dog. Funny and, being somewhat self-deprecating, it helped Dole increase his likability factor.

The humorous comeback

"Humor is the affectionate communication of insight"
—Leo Rosten

Leo Durocher was coaching first base in an exhibition game the Giants were playing at West Point. One noisy cadet kept shouting at him, trying to rattle him. At one point the cadet yelled, "How did a little squirt like you get into the major leagues?" Responded Durocher, "My Congressman appointed me!"

In the political arena, using humorous retorts is a vital skill. During a hotly contested debate, a candidate for political office rose to respond after being harshly criticized by his opponent. He said, "I'm sorry my opponent had such nasty things to say about me. I always speak well of him, but of course I suppose we could *both* be wrong."

I recall a Southern politician who was asked about the scornful comments made about him by a critic. He said, "My daddy always warned me never to wrestle with a pig. He told me we'd both get muddy, but the pig is used to it."

We call these rejoinders "perfect comebacks" because they are almost always unexpected. Criticism usually begets more criticism, but humorous retorts surpass criticism. It demonstrates the wit and character of the respondent and it can't be answered except by more humor.

A couple was watching a television soap opera when the husband became irritated by the way his wife was taking it to heart. "How can you sit there and cry about the made-up troubles of people you've never even met?" he demanded. "The same way you can jump up and scream when some guy you've never met makes a touchdown," she replied.

Responding with humor

Lou Holtz, former coach of Notre Dame's Fighting Irish football team, tells how they used to have regular media sessions during football season. These included Holtz and a couple of his players and they would answer questions about the team. During one session, the kicker got up and complained that, while most teams have at least two kickers, Notre Dame traveled with only one kicker and two priests. Why didn't they travel with two kickers and one priest? When Holtz took the platform he responded that if the kicker was more proficient they wouldn't need two priests.

Several years ago Holtz experienced a lackluster year. In spite of that the team was invited to the Sugar Bowl. Holtz went into a restaurant where he encountered a waiter who asked him, "What's the difference between Notre Dame and Cheerios?" Holtz said he didn't know. The waiter said, "Well, Cheerios belong in a bowl." The coach inquired, "What's the difference between a golf pro and me?" "I don't know," said the waiter. Holtz responded, "A golf pro leaves tips."

The rule is, the less invective, the more effective.

When rebutting critical remarks it is always nice to tailor your response by playing off the specific situation. Syndicated columnist Mark Sheilds was engaged in a debate on public television over the propriety of the president making phone calls from the White House that included solicitation of a political contribution. In defending the president, Sheilds said, "What is he supposed to do, get a pocket-full of quarters and go over to the pay phone in the Mayflower Hotel lobby?" The image of the president taking what appears to be a reasonable alternative makes the point better than simply saying, "He lives there. That's his phone!"

One of the advantages of using humor to rebut or advance an argument is that you can't contest humor with facts and figures. You can only respond effectively with more and better humor.

Former President Ronald Reagan, was known for his sense of humor and his ability to use it effectively. It was part of his so-called "Teflon presidency." One of his best lines came during his second 1984 debate with presidential contender Walter Mondale. Reagan had clearly lost the first debate and seemed confused and somewhat incoherent. There was speculation about the effect of his age on his ability to govern and to win reelection. Then, during the debate, he was asked if he thought age should be a factor in the election. His reply was classic. Said Reagan, "No I don't. And I would like to say that I will not exploit the issue of age to point out my opponent's youth and inexperience." It was a knockout punch.

Reagan, of course, went on to a second term and demonstrated his charisma throughout his presidency with the use of humor. When he was shot, he was heard to murmur to his wife, Nancy, "I should have ducked!" And when he was being placed in the ambulance, he reportedly said, "If I'd have gotten this much attention in Hollywood, I'd never have left." After arriving at the hospital he was taken to surgery where he told doctors, "I hope you're all good Republicans." This not only defused the situation for those present but very effectively sent word to the American public that he was okay.

Make it a point to notice and analyze other cases where the respondent "scored with humor." Then, the next time you're faced with a similar situation, you can draw on the humor solution. The key is to take time out from the normal course of action and evaluate how you can be more effective with a humorous approach.

Chapter Eight

Solve Problems and Deal with Adversity

"A sense of humor can help you overlook the unattractive, tolerate the unpleasant, cope with the unexpected, and smile through the unbearable."
—Anon.

Humor can indeed be helpful in solving problems. But are all problems solvable? An effective approach to dealing with problems is to first recognize that there are *only three* things we can do with any problem. You should consider this an immutable rule: The only three things we can do with any problem are 1) *get rid of it,* 2) *resolve it,* 3) *cope with it.*

Not every problem lends itself to all three solutions. Aging, for example, is a problem that cannot be resolved. Therefore, we can only deal with it by the first or third approach. We can *get rid of* the problem of aging by dying, or we can *cope with it.* Since most of us are not ready for a visit with Dr. Kervorkian, we are left to cope with growing older.

Now let's look at a typical problem we might have that lends itself to all three options. Suppose you are a manager and have an employee who is habitually late to work. You can *get rid of* the problem by dismissing the employee. You may be able to *resolve* the problem by effectively gaining the employee's cooperation. Or you can *cope with* the tardiness. Suppose you begin a lottery and have the employee's fellow workers guess what time he will arrive. Then have the employee pay one dollar to the co-worker whose guess comes the closest. This would be an example of applying the humor solution for a resolution of the problem.

Humor can help deal with life's problems by allowing us to think creatively, thereby aiding in the development of a resolution. It can help us cope with problems we have not yet resolved. Resolution usually involves getting a good perspective on the problem and thinking creatively about it. Humor gives us perspective. It can free up the mind to think "kaleidoscopically," letting the brain run wild, without regard to rationality. This free thinking process is effective in developing solutions.

Creativity

"*Lose the power to laugh and you'll lose the power to think.*"
—Anon.

All creativity is ephemeral and a product of the subconscious mind. But, for the subconscious mind to function, the conscious mind must be relaxed. Humor relaxes us and brings us into the moment. When we're laughing, we're focused on the item we're finding funny, and we are also relaxed. Try stiffening your body and then, remaining rigid, smiling broadly or laughing. It's nearly impossible to do. Amusement causes the body to relax! Relaxation is crucial to problem-solving.

Humor reduces anxiety and other obstacles that block inventiveness, thus allowing us to access our creativity and facilitating our problem-solving abilities. There have been numerous experiments where humor has been shown to stimulate creative thinking.

People who have studied creativity find that creative ideas emerge best when the problem is put aside and left for a while. As one manager said about this process, "Let's put it in a dark closet for a while and see what grows." This is how many modern gadgets and much of contemporary technology was invented. Tom Watson, legendary CEO of IBM, used to say his company was founded on "what-if thinking."

Daydreaming has led to solutions aplenty. Those little Post-It notes were invented by an engineer at 3M. When he took his new product to management they had no idea what to do with it. But they wanted to encourage this kind of inventiveness, so they were supportive and urged him to discover a use for it. It was only while singing in his church choir (relaxed and focused on something else) that he came up with the idea for sticking the notes on papers.

More recently, a mechanical engineer with IBM was trying to come up with the design of an ultraportable computer that could fit into a small square case. After months of pondering the problem, he was sitting at his desk one day daydreaming about his three-year-old daughter building shapes out of her toy blocks. Suddenly he realized that the board could be broken into two distinct, movable parts. He jumped up and rushed down the hall to a copier and made copies of his own ThinkPad. Then he sat down and began cutting them apart. By dinnertime, he had a paper prototype to show his wife. Shortly thereafter IBM had the ThinkPad 701C, a product that may set a new standard for usability among lightweight computers.

Federal Reserve chairman Alan Greenspan claims he does his best thinking in the bathtub at 5:30 in the morning. He has told friends that his IQ is about twenty points higher at this time of day when his ruminations produce "eureka moments." A scientist from Cambridge, England recently discovered the secret of how bees fly (no one had been able to figure out the aerodynamics) while sitting in his bathtub.

In all of the above cases, solutions appeared serendipitously, during periods of relaxation. This is how answers usually come to us. Thus, humor can play a valuable role in inducing relaxation, which creates an environment for creative thinking.

In-house consultants

In my own work as a put-on artist, I'm required to come up with novel ideas for spoofs tailored to the audience. This taxes my creativity because each group is different. I need to step into a convincing role the audience can relate to *and* it has to be funny. I find that my best ideas come to me when I'm showering, playing tennis, or laughing and relaxing with friends. I carry a note pad to jot down my ideas because creativity is fleeting.

I have a friend who is a former newspaper columnist and cartoonist turned screenwriter. He tells me about how those types will sit for long periods looking out the window. A new supervisor kept going by a colleague's office only to see him continually sitting there staring out the window. The supervisor announced that he wanted to hear the sounds of typewriters. He said, "I want you to be writing; that's what you're being paid for!" He was told by the writers, "When we sit down to the typewriter, it's already been written. We're putting on paper what has already been written in our heads. That's what's going on when you see us looking out the window."

Bob Thaves, whose *Frank and Ernest* cartoons appear in newspapers across the country, was hired by DuPont Corporation as an in-house spokesman for creativity. Thaves says the bureaucracy is what usually stands between creativity and expression in most organizations. DuPont wanted to encourage and stimulate creativity in its employees. So Thaves used some of his cartoons, in conjunction with employee examples of creative behavior and productivity, to illustrate creativity principles.

> *"A sense of humor reduces people and problems*
> *to their proper proportions."*
>
> —Anon.

Employers, with the help of outside consultants, are finding that their best creative resources may already be on the payroll. A recent survey conducted by a "creative consultant firm" polled 1,414 employees from more than 1,000 companies and found that workers and managers believe their organizations are operating on less than half their collective brainpower. Companies such as AT&T, Kimberly-Clark and even NASA are hiring these so-called "innovation and critical thinking experts." The idea is to free the creative spirit and stimulate employees' critical thinking so they can make the imaginative leap between problem identification and solution. They have found that ideas flow faster if people are in a playful frame of mind. Thus, they are using such things as Silly Putty and Play-Doh, as well as humor, to help employees become better problem solvers.

Humor-based solutions

Sometimes creative problem solving follows the Judo/Aikido principle. Such was the case when, in the 1940s, Dwight D. Eisenhower was president of Columbia University. A problem he faced was that students ignored sidewalks and trampled the grass. No matter how many "Keep Off the Grass" signs were put up, and no matter how many fences were erected, the students would still take whatever routes they found convenient as they hurried from one building to another.

Footpaths were worn along these routes, and administrators despaired over the appearance of the campus. Eisenhower's solution: Forget the signs and fences and install sidewalks where the footpaths had been worn. Then remove the unused sidewalks and plant grass there instead. It worked because he moved with the flow.

Now let's look at the same technique but accented with an amusing twist. Black belts at situational Judo know how to punctuate their moves with humor.

During the Spanish-American War, the Navy christened two ships the *Harvard* and the *Yale*. The Navy brass liked the idea so much that when Admiral Dewey captured the Spanish fleet, he was instructed to rename the seized ships after American colleges. The admiral didn't agree with this but knew that wouldn't carry water with his superiors. So he wired the Navy Department his choices for the first two ships: the *Massachusetts Institute of Technology* and the *Vermont Normal College for Women*. The Navy dropped the idea of a "college fleet." Can you see how he attacked the idea by embracing it? The technique here is to go along rather than resist, then exaggerate to make your point. By taking a ridiculous idea to its extreme in a humorous vein, you expose its ludicrousness. This works much better than a more resistant "That's silly!" You sneak up on them and make your point in a way that displays the folly of the idea you oppose.

> *"The crisis of today is the joke of tomorrow."*
> —H.G. Wells

Here's another example: At the Constitutional Convention, someone proposed limiting the U.S. standing army to 5,000 men. George Washington responded by requesting a clause that would limit the size of any invading army to 3,000 troops. Laughter followed and the proposal was abandoned.

At other times, what might be needed is some friendly, humorous prodding. A construction company had a problem getting employees to turn in time cards at the end of the week. After trying a number of solutions they turned to humor and that did the trick. They announced that anyone who didn't turn in their time card must walk through the office in their underwear the following week. This was kicked off by the office manager who came up with the idea. She paraded through the office in a pair of bloomers and made it work by showing her own willingness to perform the act while, at the same time, displaying her sense of humor.

Unintentional humor

Sometimes the solution is so creative as to be unintentionally humorous. Such was the case of the problem of guests absconding with White House silverware following monthly luncheons with journalists. President Kennedy became frustrated and asked his press secretary, Pierre Salinger, what could be done about it. Salinger recruited a professional pickpocket to attend the luncheons and recover pilfered silverware.

In all cases, the creative juices have to get flowing for solutions to occur. The award-winning advertising agency Carmichael-Lynch knows how to set the mood for creativity at its Minneapolis headquarters. There you'll find forty-one conference rooms, each with its own theme. Agricultural accounts are discussed in the "Cow Room," where they sit around a table that is a piece of glass atop a full feed bin in chairs that look like Holsteins and have tails. Graffiti, a chain-link fence and a basketball hoop cover the walls of the "Urban Room." When account executives want to create ads for clients, they do it in a mood-setting environment.

Making obstacles into opportunities

Sometimes negative publicity can be ballyhooed into a buildup. When the Chicago Bears football team was scheduled to play the Minnesota Vikings at the new Metrodome, Bears' coach Mike Ditka was outspoken in his dislike of the site. The Metrodome, he complained, was better suited for roller skating than football.

Mary Horwath, Public Relations and Advertising Director of Rollerblade, heard about Ditka's remark, gathered her sense of humor and swung into action. She personally delivered sets of her skates to Vikings' cheerleaders and sent a pair to Ditka.

The *NFL Today* pregame show featured Ditka skating around his office (he has a sense of humor too!) on his single-row, wheeled Rollerblades.

As the game got underway, the Vikings' cheerleaders were seen on national television wearing their new skates as well — with an explanation, of course. All this television coverage was augmented by widespread newspaper reporting.

Horwath had taken a lemon and made lemonade. She estimated the publicity was worth about a quarter of a million dollars.

On another occasion, in what was most likely an unintentionally humorous spontaneous remark, Ditka is reported to have closed one of his pregame locker room pep talks by shouting, "All right, let's say the Lord's Prayer and get the hell out of here!"

From lemons to lemonade

Another example of going with the flow and punctuating it with humor is the case of Indiana University. Not the one in Bloomington, Indiana, but the one in Indiana, Pennsylvania. Known as IUP, the school was the subject of an item in a book which named their campus as having the ugliest male student body. Rather than protest, the university's PR people decided to go with the flow, adding an accent of humor.

T-shirts suddenly appeared on campus with slogans such as "Ugly and Proud of It!" and "IUP Men — The Few, The Proud & the Ugly." Then an Ugly Man contest was held. Newspapers around the country covered this self-deprecating approach, and the school got tons of publicity. The result was a dramatic increase in the university's appeal at high school college fairs, resulting in elevated enrollments. When faced with a problem — especially a formidable one — consider going with the flow, and help your solution by trying to *think funny*!

The fashionable Hillcrest Country Club in Los Angeles posted a sign prohibiting cigar smoking. Comedian George Burns, a club member who was then 95, protested. The next day a new sign went up: "Cigar Smoking Prohibited for Anyone Under 95."

Creative solutions

Oftentimes a creative solution is not just prompted by humorous musing. Rather, the very solution is grounded in humor. I remember reading about a motorist who, while driving along a California highway, saw a neatly dressed young man who appeared to be a hitchhiking college student, holding a sign that read, "Stop at Joe's, 100 yards ahead." About a football field's length down the ramp stood another young man with a sign that read, "Joe's." These fellows had figured out how to get around the problem of getting a ride in these scary times by putting their sense of humor to work!

A similar tactic was used by a homeless fellow who survives on his sense of humor and apparently subscribes to truth in advertising. He sits along a busy street in San Diego with a hand-lettered sign that reads:

HELP!
My Blood-Alcohol Level
Is Dangerously Low!
Donations Accepted

When a would-be robber came to his window at a San Diego branch of Bank of America and handed him a note demanding 50s and 100s in cash — written on a Wells Fargo deposit slip — the teller was unflappable and thought funny. He said, "I'm sorry, but you'll need a B of A withdrawal slip." The stunned gunman bolted. Some spontaneous funny thinking had foiled the robber and averted a crime. I'm not recommending this as a standard course of action in unpredictable situations. It does, however, illustrate how thinking funny proved successful in this particular case.

During a strike of New York city garbagemen some years ago, I read about a man who got rid of his trash by gift wrapping it and leaving it in plain view in the back seat of his unlocked car. He claimed that every time he returned to his car, his garbage was gone! This may seem a frivolous story, but it has some lessons. After all, the essence of this book is to help you think funny and transfer ideas to your personal situations. The primary lesson is: If you want to get rid of something, pretend you're trying to protect it. People will think it's valuable, and someone will steal it! A friend of mine attended a talk I gave several years ago when I shared this story with my audience. Several weeks later he got a new water tank for his home. Not knowing what to do with the old one, he recalled this story and used some lateral thinking to transfer the idea to his own situation. He got the box the new water tank came in, placed the old one in it, taped it up as if new, and leaned it against his house. Several days later it had disappeared. Some lucky person was now the proud owner of a completely worn-out water tank!

Making stumbling blocks into stepping stones

Some other examples of putting the humor solution to work: When the "mad cow" scare hit England, sales of British beef plummeted. So Harry Goode, a dairy farmer who realized he would no longer be able to make a profit on his older cows, turned them into four-legged billboards. He mounted ads on the bovines where they graze beside the busy highway outside Birmingham, selling rights to the flanks of eight Bessies for about $40 per cow per week. One of his first customers was Ben & Jerry's Ice Cream. A little bit of funny thinking provided a profit and a way out of a disastrous situation.

Television host Hugh Downs tells the story of his father, Milton, and how he dealt with some of the problems of being poor during the Depression. The

146

family was sitting in their car getting ready to leave for church one Sunday when a bill collector drove up to the house. Telling his family to wait in the car, Milton joined the man at his front door and asked, "Do you think anyone's home?" When the stranger said he didn't think so, Milton agreed and they both walked off the porch and drove away. Again, thinking funny carried the day.

A business executive felt that unexpected guests were depriving her of precious time. So she devised a defense based on some humorous thinking. Now, when her doorbell rings, she puts on her hat and coat before she opens the door. If it's someone she doesn't want to see, she says, "Oh, isn't this too bad! I'm just on my way out." If it's someone she wants to see, she says, "What great timing! I just got in!"

Another woman, annoyed with constant telemarketing calls, came up with a humorous but effective way to deal with them. When she recognizes the sales approach, she feigns a sigh of relief and blurts out, "Oh thank God. You want to sell me something! Great! I thought it was another of those calls from the pesky collection agencies."

An elderly lady in the San Francisco area finally got tired of having to stand up throughout her trips on the BART (Bay Area Rapid Transit system). So, thinking funny, she devised a solution. She carried a cane on board. Then she would approach a young man who was seated, hand him her cane and ask him if he would hold it so she could hang on to the ceiling rails with both hands. Most people would immediately stand and give her their seat.

More problem-solving maneuvers

When I was a youngster in the navy we would go on liberty and carouse all night, so by the afternoon of the next day we were quite tired. A friend and I devised a method of catching up on our rest during the workday. We would get a can of paint, along with the attendant supplies, then go to the bunk area where we'd crawl under a stack of bunks, leaving the paint can and supplies beside us. There we caught up on our sleep, but anyone passing by would see our feet sticking out, observe the paint supplies and conclude we were under there painting.

Some professional speakers like to talk with fellow passengers when flying to engagements, while others prefer to prepare for their presentations or just enjoy the peace and quiet of a book. When I don't want to be bothered on an airplane, I take along one of those earplugs that normally connects to a radio or tape recorder. Although I don't have the recorder, I just plug it into my ear and put the other end in my pocket. No one knows the difference, and I'm left undisturbed.

147

Famous hoaxer Hugh Troy used his skills at practical joking to serve his own purposes in solving problems, while having some fun in the process. After college, Troy decided to be an artist and moved to New York City. Shortly after he arrived, an art exhibition featuring the works of Vincent Van Gogh came to the Museum of Modern Art. Troy was eager to see it but realized he would have to fight an enormous crowd. He suspected that the spectators would be more attracted by legends about Van Gogh's personal life than his art — particularly his slicing off his ear and sending it to a prostitute.

Using his sense of humor and his skills at practical joking, he got some dried beef and carved it into a fake ear which he mounted on a plaque. On the plaque he put an inscription that read, "This is the ear that Van Gogh cut off and sent to his mistress on December 24, 1888." He smuggled it into the museum and put it up on the wall. The next day he found most of the crowd gathered around his masterpiece, leaving the other works of art for him to enjoy.

I once had a neighbor who decided to redo his front-lawn. He dug it up but then got busy with other projects. For months it remained that way with large piles of dirt beside a number of holes. I finally sent him a letter, ostensibly from the homeowners association, telling him he had won an award for the most unique lawn design in the community. While the association was not sure what the design represented, I wrote, we guessed it was a replica of Dusselldorf, Germany after an allied bombing. He knew it was me who had sent the letter and he laughed about it more than once. He also completed his front-lawn project.

I recall one story of a little fellow seated on an airplane next to a big, strapping tough-looking guy. While his seatmate slept, the little man became airsick and vomited all over the big guy. What to do? "Boy," he thought, "when he wakes up is he going to be mad!" But thinking funny saved the day. When the hulk awoke the smaller man looked at him and said, "Are you feeling better now?"

Coping

It is not so simple to get rid of most problems and most problems don't lend themselves to easy resolutions. Usually we are left to cope with them. A professional speaker, who was a downed pilot during the Vietnam War, talks about his time in the "Hanoi Hilton," the infamous Vietnamese prison camp. He explains how humor helped him and his fellow prisoners cope with the grim life. He relates how the shower had a little sign that said, "Smile, you're on Candid Camera!"

Of all the many examples of using humor as a coping device, one of the most profound is described in Viktor Frankl's book, *Man's Search for Meaning*. This gripping book chronicles the author's years at Auschwitz and other Nazi prison camps. Dr. Frankl found meaning in life despite tremendous suffering. While the book illustrates the cruelty, pain and horror of life in a concentration camp, the focus is on Frankl's use of his experience to survive.

He calls humor a "weapon of the soul" and explains how he and a fellow inmate survived through humor. They made a pact and every day each invented at least one amusing story to tell the other. Sometimes they imagined retaining the habits of prison life after their liberation. Their diet consisted mostly of potato soup — actually water with a few potato pieces on the bottom. So they would always ask the person serving the soup to get it "from the bottom." They imagined how, after their release, they would attend a fashionable dinner party and ask the hostess to ladle the soup "from the bottom."

Dr. Frankl says humor, more than anything in the human makeup, allows us to rise above any situation, even if only for a short time. Developing a sense of humor is a trick you learn in mastering the art of living, he says.

Christopher Reeves tells about his ordeal of being paralyzed and unable to breathe without a ventilator. He was lying in the hospital one bleak day feeling helpless when the door flew open and a fellow in a surgical gown wearing glasses and speaking with a Russian accent hurried in. He told Reeves he was a proctologist and had to examine him immediately. Reeves says his first thought was that they were giving him way too many drugs. But he soon discovered it was his old friend Robin Williams spoofing him. Says Reeves, "For the first time since the accident, I laughed." He adds that it gave him hope for recovery.

"In prehistoric times, mankind often had only two choices in crisis situations: fight or flee. In modern times, humor offers a third alternative: fight, flee or laugh."
—Robert Orben

Turning to humor in disaster

I believe that disaster is kind of a litmus test for the existence of a sense of humor. Actress Shirley MacLaine defended her home from a wildfire roaring out of the mountains above the Pacific Coast. It was the tenth time her Malibu home had been threatened by fire. She was interviewed by a television reporter while she and her tenants were spending the evening watering down the roof of her building as burning cinders fell. Quipped MacLaine, "I do think they ought to change the area code and make it 911."

Over and over again, we read about how people used their sense of humor to deal with disaster. Following the big earthquake in Los Angeles a few years ago, a house was put up for sale in a neighborhood where the quake had wreaked havoc. Below the For Sale sign was the message: "Some Assembly Required." In a similar case, a Minnesota man whose car had been crushed by a huge tree trunk during a tornado was seen standing next to his car waving to passing motorists. On his car was a hand-lettered sign that read, "Compact Car." Residents of Grand Forks, North Dakota, suffered the devastation of a major flood in 1997. During the messy business of cleaning up afterward, their sense of humor about the matter came through in their lingo. For example, "flood tan" denoted the brown strip of skin from the point where the rubber gloves ended to where the T-shirts began. What appeared to be endless meetings of the city council were deemed "Buns of Steel," and a "flood moment" was temporarily spacing out ("Sorry, I was having a flood moment.")

"Humor provides us with a valuable tool for maintaining an inner strength in the midst of outer turmoil."

—Brian Deery

Perhaps all these folks discovered that it is impossible to laugh and worry at the same time! That comes to mind when I recall baseball player John Kruk of the Phillies who had his cancerous testicle removed. When he returned to the team after recovering, he wore a T-shirt with the words: "If you don't let me play, I'm taking my ball and going home." A little humor helps calm the mind so you can think more clearly. During the Cuban missile crisis, President Kennedy reportedly asked for a joke to open a meeting where they would be brainstorming for solutions. As the debate progressed there was discussion of deposing Castro and someone jokingly proposed making Bobby Kennedy mayor of Havana.

I also heard about an occasion when Sylvester Stallone and his entourage were flying to Cannes, France. About two and a half hours after takeoff from Miami and well out to sea, the pilot-side windshield on the private Gulfstream jet blew out for unexplained reasons. Nobody was hurt, but it was a frightening incident. Stallone displayed his sense of humor by commenting, "I always wanted to travel to Europe in a convertible."

The therapeutic value of laughter was also demonstrated during a flood in Iowa. The *Des Moines Register* ran an "I'm a Floody Mess" contest, trying to keep the city's spirits up after the water system failed. Subscribers completing joke sentences would win prizes. In touting the campaign, the newspaper announced, "Attention, unwashed Iowans: Convert your body odor into cash!" Contestants were to finish sentences such as "I smell so bad . . . ." or "My clothes are so dirty . . ." The lesson is clear — if you can't get rid of the problem or solve it, why not adjust your attitude to make the best of it?

Humor can make the unbearable bearable

"The next best thing to solving a problem is finding some humor in it"
—Frank A. Clark

In June, 1997, a long-awaited heavyweight championship boxing match took place in Las Vegas between Evander Holyfield and Mike Tyson. People flocked to the MGM Hotel and Casino for ringside seats and millions paid $50 each to watch it on pay-per-view television. It ended in the third round when Tyson was disqualified after biting Holyfield's ear for the second time. After this bizarre conclusion to the fight, the public's disgust was shown by a plethora of bad but funny punnery. Among them: "Talk about a hungry fighter!" "A man's gotta eat!"

The plays on the word "ear" were plentiful and outrageous: "Tyson's ex-wife told him, 'Please don't nibble my ears.' " "Tyson is looking for a bout with Ross Perot. The little guy's reply: 'I'm all ears.' " Holyfield was said to have been "ear-itated," and the bout was reported to usher in a new "ear-a" in boxing. The digs just kept coming: "Pay Per Chew television," "Jaws IV," and headlines such as, "Tyson's Behavior Hard To Swallow." Hollywood's Wax Museum even moved their statue of Tyson from the Sports Hall of Fame to the Chamber of Horrors and placed it next to Hannibal "the Cannibal" Lecter, of *Silence of the Lambs* fame.

"You can turn painful situations around through laughter. If you can find humor in anything, you can survive it."
—Bill Cosby

Checkers Drive-In restaurants, a chain that operates 485 restaurants in 23 states began airing commercials for its Champ burger that spoofed the boxing incident. The theme of one: "Hey Mike, next time you bite a Champ, at least get some fries." Humorous posters appeared satirizing the event and participants surfaced. The Postal Service reported that they delivered to Tyson a dozen five inch-long genuine fleshy pig's ears, stamped and addressed as post cards. Finally, a North Hollywood confectioner, Frank Sheftel, owner of the Candy Factory, produced and sold ear-shaped chocolates with fake teeth marks calling them, "Earvander-Tyson Bites."

When such dark episodes occur, the American public takes it from loathing to the trivial by using the humor solution. The aftermath of the humor was that the initial outrage which had provided boxing with a black eye, actually created an incredible resurgence of interest in the sport.

151

Ashland Oil Co. earned brickbats from angry residents after one of its storage tanks spilled a large amount of oil into a river near Pittsburgh. It seemed that everyone in the vicinity had ill feelings about it — except one person. In its employee newsletter the company reprinted a letter from a little girl that read, "Dear Ashland Oil Co.: I know a lot of people are in grief because they did not have any water. But I want to thank you because I did not have to go to school. My brother thanks you, too. He did not have to take a bath." By poking a little fun at itself, the company diminished some of the stressful feelings of its employees.

Humor and tension

Remember that humor is a relaxant; and don't forget to call on it when you are feeling pressured. My friend Tom is a teaching tennis professional. He told me that he was recently given the task of teaching a rather large group. Since he is accustomed to working one-on-one, he was a bit anxious about it. The students, all teenagers, were obviously nervous too. So, recalling what I had told him about using humor to relax, he began by telling them that he wouldn't remember their names. He explained that there were only three things he was not good at remembering: Names, places and, well . . . he couldn't remember the third thing. They all laughed. He told me later he could actually feel the tension diminish.

Dr. Jolene Kriett is a transplant specialist at the University of California at San Diego. She is second in command of their heart and lung transplant program — one of the busiest and most efficient in the country. She says a sense of humor helps in her work by breathing some relief into the lives of her patients. In the recovery room, following a double lung transfer she used her dry wit to calm fears and relieve tension. In front of her patient, Kriett deadpanned to another doctor, "Wait a minute, are you sure we put the good lungs in?"

Stand-up dentistry

Dr. John Lauer is a San Diego dentist who has a reputation for joking his way through a successful practice of "drill, fill and bill." According to an article written about him he uses a stand-up dentist style. He asks patients why gas station cash registers are open but the restrooms are locked. Following that up, he tells them he was going to buy a copy of "The Power of Positive Thinking," but says, "What good would that do?"

Take a page from Dr. Frankl and use humor to deal with recurring stressful situations in your life. Driving, for example, can be very stressful, especially if you happen to live in a large city with congested highways. Even if you don't, driving exposes you to rude and inconsiderate behavior. People who cut you off or who won't let you into their lane can cause stress. I am always taken aback by those who do not use their turn signals — or who put them on during the turn — as if they are somehow connected to their steering mechanisms and help the cars change direction. Seeing the humor will automatically diminish the stress. It helps to think of the ironies in driving. We are all told, for example, to keep lots of space between us and the car in front of us. Try doing that and watch how any such space is immediately consumed by other cars slipping into it.

There is a joke about a new citizen taking a driving test and being asked what to do at a traffic light. "That's easy," was the reply. "For red, you stop; for green, you go and yellow means speed up."

"We don't laugh because we feel good; we feel good because we laugh."
— Bob Ross

Medical research has shown that laughing triggers production of the body's "natural painkillers." But the emotional lift we get from humor in these situations may be more crucial than the biochemical ones. Making a joke of your situation puts you on top of it emotionally.

A nurse from Louisville, Kentucky, tells about a woman who suffers from a rare chronic illness that affects the connective tissue. Rushed to the hospital after an attack that was life-threatening, she was met by a hospital clerk who told her, "I'm terribly sorry, but we don't take emergency cases here." The clerk handed her a walking map to the nearest hospital which had little footprint diagrams that reminded her of the ones Arthur Murray used to teach the rumba. At the bottom it said, "This map not to scale." She said she knew that someday she'd find it funny.

Laughter is our stress management tool

Writer Lawrence Eisenberg wrote a piece about his ordeal with prostate cancer. Following surgery, as is the norm, he experienced incontinence. Using his sense of humor to cope, he envisioned an airline called "Incontinental Airlines, with a commode under every seat."

The ability to see the funny side; to appreciate the ridiculous in life and to laugh at our troubles is one of the greatest assets one can possess. It is fundamental to complete mental health. A humorous perspective allows us to look at life in a healthy and vigorous way. Like love, compassion, understanding and courage, a humorous attitude can help sustain us through good times and bad. It can lighten the load of our daily routine and responsibilities. It can help us through suffering and pain and even enable us to live joyous lives in the worst of times.

153

Research on the relationship between a sense of humor and mental health supports the view that humor is an important component of healthy mental and emotional adjustment. The level of an individual's ability to appreciate humor is an indication of one's degree of mental maturity and emotional health. Conversely, the absence of a sense of humor, or a limited reaction to humor, is an indicator of inhibition or a restrictive lifestyle. The humorous perspective is the ultimate achievement in the quest for happiness and good mental soundness.

Properly managed stress gives us extra courage, energy and the strength needed to successfully cope with problems. It can give us the competitive edge that's necessary for peak performance. It's also therapeutic! In his bestselling book, *Anatomy of an Illness*, author Norman Cousins related his own experience of using laughter to cure what doctors had said was an incurable ailment. Not only did he credit humor with helping his recovery, but he said he made the joyous discovery that ten minutes of genuine belly laughter had an anesthetic effect and would give him at least two hours of pain-free sleep.

Mind-body magic

Largely as a result of Norman Cousins' experience, a new branch of medicine called psychoneuroimmunology (PNI) has emerged. It deals with the interactions between the brain, the endocrine system and the immune system. Much has been written on this subject, but the bottom line is that positive feelings can dramatically impact our health. An estimated one half of medical schools now offer some sort of mind-body instruction. The so-called "relaxation response" can treat insomnia, hypertension, infertility and other ills claims Dr. Herbert Benson of Boston's Deaconess Hospital. He is setting up affiliates of his Mind/Body Medical Institute at hospitals across the country. Of course, as mentioned above, stress is behind much of modern illness.

Certain kinds of stress can weaken the body's immune system and set the stage for disease. Similarly, relieving stress and depression can help the body mount its defenses to avert sickness and recover from illnesses. The ability of the body to turn back illness is one of the wonders of the world. Interestingly, it is possible for people to *summon* positive attitudes or emotions to create desired effects. Thus, the mind can, in large part, control a person's health.

Humor and the nervous system

Harvard Medical School students were tested for immunoglobulins — an index to the immune function — before and after viewing an amusing film. The study showed a measurable increase in the immunoglobulins following the laughter. Conversely, researchers at Ohio State University were able to show that apprehension over grades as examination time approached could actually impair the immune system. All this has dispelled the previously held scientific notion that the central nervous system and the systems that control the immune and endocrine functions are separate. Research on PNI continues and could change the face of biomedicine within the decade.

"Snow and adolescence are the only problems that disappear if you ignore them long enough."
—Earl Wilson

In the meantime, using what we already know can help us cope with and defeat stress. Facial expressions, for example, not only mirror our emotions — expressing what is going on inside — but can also help *change* our mood in ways that assist in handling a variety of situations. A broad smile, for instance, gives us an "oxygen bath" (which is why the face gets flushed), causing a sense of euphoria. Laughter has a similar and even more pronounced effect.

Hearty laugh and healthy heart

Studies show you can even fake it and it will work — albeit not as well as a genuine laugh. The point is, we don't laugh because we feel good. We feel good because we laugh! Laughing involves the respiratory, cardiovascular, muscular, endocrine and central nervous systems. When we laugh, heart rate, blood pressure and other measures of bodily activity speed up. Afterward, these physiological measurements sink below the previous levels.

That's why we relax so deeply following a hearty laugh. As Dr. Lee Berk, a professor of pathology and laboratory medicine at Loma Linda University says, "If we took what we now know about laughter and bottled it, it would require FDA approval." Norman Cousins called laughter a "massage from the inside." No wonder Zen Buddhists believe if you start every morning with prolonged laughter it will take care of the rest of your day!

Adversity

Adversity brings out the humor in those who truly have a sense of humor. Robert Polhill was held hostage by Lebanese extremists for more than three years. It was particularly difficult for him because, as a diabetic, he had trouble getting insulin from his captors who didn't speak his language. Upon his release he discovered he had throat cancer and had to have his voice box removed.

155

Without a job, breathing through a hole in his neck, he wrote on a yellow pad, "I'll talk again, but I'm a realist, too. I'll never have another hit record."

Life is full of problems. They are, in fact, what propel us through life. Without them, we would feel unfulfilled. Yet very little is taught about the approaches to dealing successfully with problems. Perhaps less known is the priceless value of humor in the role of addressing problems that confront us. In your own troubled times, turn to the magic of mirth to help you through them.

"Time heals everything . . . except a leaky faucet."

—Anon.

Chapter Nine

Strengthen the Bonds of Friendship and Romance

"Among those whom I like or admire, I can find no common denominator, but among those whom I love, I can: all of them make me laugh"
—W.H. Auden

Romance is basically a strong friendship with the added dimension of intimacy. Love relationships incorporate many of the same elements of a good friendship and allow your humor to work for you in many of the same ways. Just as you *connect* with people through humor, so you will connect with your romantic partner. Humor and laughter are shared experiences. As such they are bonding devices. Humor also helps keep the channels of communication open. This is a vital element of any relationship.

Have you ever gone to a party or other social event and walked into the room not knowing what group or person to join? Imagine the setting: A room full of small groups of people, all engaged in conversation, but one group is laughing. Doesn't it act as a magnet, drawing you to it? That is the place you want to be because those people are having fun, and folks are drawn to fun. People are drawn to those of the opposite sex — as well as their own sex — by the fun factor.

"Making it fun" applies to personal relationships as well as other situations. When queried about the kind of man they want, women consistently name a sense of humor as their top priority. Friendships and romantic relationships between healthy people are usually full of fun, playfulness and laughter.

According to a survey in *Modern Bride* magazine, only fifteen percent of women said looks were among the three main virtues they wanted in a man.

The most important were honesty, shared values and a sense of humor, followed by intelligence and kindness. Only two percent mentioned money and twenty-nine percent said if they could change one thing about a man it would be his personality. While I have not seen any actual statistics on men's perceptions of women, my own empirical research shows similar results.

Humor in meeting people

Following my divorce several years ago, I placed ads in the personals of the newspapers as a method of meeting new women. I found that humor would endear them to me faster than anything else. Tasteful humor was magnetic at every level of the process which includes the ad itself, the initial phone conversation and the actual meeting — if one occurred.

In talking with the many women I met through this method, I found that most of them considered the process laborious, stressful and frustrating. But I looked upon it as an adventure. While meeting people was disappointing and frustrating at times, the overall experience was pleasant.

Meeting women through personal ads, as well as the more traditional ways, has been a great opportunity to use whatever humor skills I possess. Since I travel frequently, I am sometimes dilatory in returning calls made as a result of my own ad in the personals. Sometimes when I would call someone after having been out of town for a while they would say, "Gosh, I called you several weeks ago!" I would reply, "Well I'm sorry but I just got out of jail." While some would hang up on me, it was a good way to weed out the humor-impaired.

Other occasions arose when it was necessary to introduce myself on the telephone. Women would sometimes ask what I did in my spare time. I'd reply that I used my chemistry set to develop vaccines for Ebola and other deadly diseases in third-world countries. I would add that, in any time left over, I worked with handicapped animals. One of three things would happen when I did this. Some women would laugh. Others did not laugh because they just didn't get it; or, if they did get it, they were offended or were not amused. I suspected the women who fell into the last two categories would not make a good match for me.

Apparently, I'm not the only one who recognizes the attraction of humor. I read about an ad in the personals column of a Connecticut newspaper that read: "Ugly, rude, insincere, untrustworthy, dishonest, slovenly, uneducated single male, 24, hopes to entice exact opposite single female, 20-28 with romantic candlelight dinner."

This is the magic of humor. Nothing can replace it when it is used properly. Incidentally, even though most women list a sense of humor as the trait most desired in a mate, very few of the women I met were able to convince me they had one. That's the problem with using humor as a criterion. Since everyone thinks they have a good sense of humor, asking them about this sixth sense is meaningless. You must find ways to measure it objectively — to the extent possible — since humor is quite subjective. If you agree with my own definition of a sense of humor, put them to the test: Can they laugh at themselves? Can they think funny? This may not be discoverable at once; it may take two or more meetings to determine this.

Severely humor-impaired

When I would set up a meeting with a lady, I'd tell her, "You'll easily recognize me. I'll be wearing lime green slacks with a pink striped shirt with a yellow polka dot tie." Of course I wouldn't really be dressed that way. The tie would be picked to match the slacks. In one case, I had asked my date to meet me at the cocktail lounge of a nice restaurant I frequent. She told me she didn't like to walk into strange places by herself and asked me to meet her in the vestibule. I arrived a few minutes early and told everybody from the parking valet to the bartender to welcome my new acquaintance by name as if she were a regular there. They did as I asked and it was amusing to watch her as the host and others greeted her by name and asking why she hadn't been there lately. At first she was astonished but quickly caught on and found it quite amusing. She seemed to appreciate that I had made the effort to add a little fun to the evening.

On another occasion I did the same thing with a date. Her reaction was totally different. She seemed to be offended and sneered at the personnel who called her by name. My initial reaction to her behavior proved to be correct. I soon discovered the poor soul was severely humor-impaired.

Once in a relationship, humor can be an adhesive to help cement it. A sense of humor can be used to maintain interest and to achieve specific goals. When I hadn't seen a certain friend for a while, I took one of those notices you get in the mail about missing persons, took her photo, sized it properly at one of those copy machines that adjust a photo's dimensions, and pasted it over the photos on the piece and sent it to her. You can also do this with a milk carton. I've also pasted photos over those on supermarket tabloids and sent them to friends.

I believe that a sense of humor is one of the personality traits most attractive to members of the opposite sex. Humor is a kind of secret communication that serves as an emotional nurturance. It has a relaxing effect and allows people to get into a playful mood which facilitates romance.

Humor in marriage

Nearly everyone is emotionally close and "in love" when they get married. The trick is to feel the same about each other fifteen years later. Here again, humor can assist by keeping the relationship interesting and fun. Studies show that long-term successful marriages normally contain three elements: The two people are best friends, have mutual respect, and laugh a lot and have fun together.

Ideally, marriage should grow into the ultimate relationship encompassing all the wonderful elements of a friendship along with romance, including sexual attraction, affection and devotion. As long as you can laugh together, you will probably be able to cope and persevere. It helps us lighten up on ourselves and annoying situations and to be less judgmental and self-righteous about others. Humor and playfulness will help you over the rough spots in relationships.

Muscleman Arnold Schwarzennegger is a conservative Republican. Many were surprised when he married Maria Shriver of the liberal Kennedy clan. But they surmount their political differences by kidding each other about it. Schwarzennegger jokes that, when he took his marriage vows to care for Maria in sickness and in health, he told her that being a Democrat fell under the sickness category.

"Laughter between two is sometimes a closer act of love than any other."
—Oswald Wynd

Humorous marriage proposals, such as those on sports arena scoreboards and blimp trailers, indicate a bond of fun and friendship. Other original proposals include a treasure hunt that culminates with the big question or finding the ring on a dessert tray at a fancy restaurant. I recently read of a novel case where the 27-year-old man enlisted the help of the puzzle editor of the *New York Times* to create a crossword puzzle encoded with his proposal. The bride-to-be, an avid crossword devotee, sat across from her beau over brunch working the puzzle, only to realize from the answers that he was asking her to marry him.

Some people instill humor in the ceremony. My daughter and her husband had considered inserting language in the marriage vows to include lowering the toilet seat and replacing the cap on the toothpaste. When Nobel Prizewinning chemist Kary Mullins wed artist Nancy Lier Cosgrove (both had been married several times before) their hand-crafted vows included the promise "to stay together long enough to justify this big party."

When Jane Wise set the wedding date with her partner, Harold Smart, the invitation read: "We invite you to celebrate the Wise choice this Smart man has made . . . ."

Here's an actual wedding invitation I received: (Names have been changed.)

To the total amazement and consternation
of the Western Hemisphere
Deborah Applebee and Leonard Pritchard
are entering into the Sanctity of Holy Matrimony

(ha ha ha)
Your presence is respectfully requested
The gala event will be held at 7:02 P.M.
on Saturday, January 14, 1989, at the
Tuolumne River Lodge, Modesto, California USA
Please confirm your RSVP
within the next forty-five minutes
or this notice will self destruct
Dinner of sorts will be served at
7:16 p.m. and drinks will be
distributed to the first 300 guests only.
(you snooze you loose — no booze)
Entertainment will be provided by the
Boston Pops Orchestra
Directed by Professor Who's Who
For fear of receiving a duplication
in gifts, we are requesting "cash"*
only, and lots of it! If you are
unable to attend, send the cash anyway.

*We will accept Hong Kong Dollars

Here's another actual wedding invitation I saw:

Cookie "I never will marry" Caminarro

and

Richard "Once is enough" Hollingsworth

invite you to join them

in "eating their words."

Some innovative couples take a novel approach when planning their nuptials. Ralph Padgett met his bride Gia Serrano at a drug store and soda fountain. So when they decided to marry they selected that same place for the ceremony. Another couple who met while shopping at a convenience store decided on that venue as their marriage site. As their guests sipped Slurpees and Big Gulps, the bride walked down the snack-food aisle. The good news was the guests had no trouble finding rice to throw. Musician Kenny Loggins claims he and his wife Julia exchanged their marriage vows in the nude. He says it was meant as a statement that they had nothing to hide. While oftentimes the setting signifies some aspect of the relationship, some couples simply want to do it a little differently. My friend, Cork Proctor is a Las Vegas comedian. His marriage took place at a casino and had a Gay Nineties theme. All guests came dressed in clothes of that era. He slid down a fire station type pole to recite the wedding vows.

"Love may make the world go round,
but it's laughter that keeps us from getting dizzy."
—Donald Zochert

Another couple rode Asian and African elephants down the Atlantic City boardwalk (the origin of the elephants apparently matched the origin of the couple) to a bungee jumping platform. They had their ceremony on the platform and then jumped together over the Atlantic for the vows. Said the groom: "I wanted my wedding to be special. When I'm flying through the air holding her in my arms and knowing she trusts me 100 percent, that is what love is all about." There seems to be no end to the unusual nuptial settings people will come up with. San Diego's Sea World began a dolphin interaction program that allows people to learn and mingle with the sea creatures. So Philip Leone and his fiancee Janna O'Dell bought all 10 places in one session and exchanged their marriage vows in the pool with two dolphins as the wedding party. With good humor, the minister donned a wet suit and stepped into the shallow end of the pool.

When NBA star Gary Payton wed Monique James they made the San Francisco wedding quite a trip. The groom and his groomsmen emerged from a fleet of six vintage Rolls Royces. Their black suede shoes were embroidered with a basketball and net and when it came time to place the ring on her finger, teammate Nate McMillan began a thirteen-man passing of the colossal diamond to Payton — signifying the essence of their sport. The point is to do it with a little pizzazz!

When Jean Andrews and Skeet Freelove planned their wedding a compromise was in order. They were coming from different backgrounds. She was a Republican fund-raiser and he was a cowboy and professional rodeo rider. She wanted to take the vows in San Diego and he longed for his native Texas. So they flew some Texas dirt into San Diego to stand on. She wanted a champagne toast; he wanted shots of tequila, so they went for both. They registered for gifts at a tack and feed store as well as a more traditional retailer. The honeymoon was a week in the Colorado wilderness and then on to Hawaii for some sun and surfing. Compromise shouldn't be a problem in the relationship.

Special occasions

Couples who can approach relationships with a humorous outlook are more likely to be successful in their marriage. Besides being an excellent aphrodisiac, humor will serve to defuse marital conflicts by smoothing out some of those ripples before they become tidal waves and providing an outlet when the options seem to be homicide or divorce.

Birthdays are excellent opportunities to have some fun with friends and family. When my wife turned forty, I had a party for her that was fashioned after a funeral. The announcement took the format and appearance of a funeral notice. Guests were requested to come attired in whatever they were wearing when they got out of bed. Black arm bands were furnished at the door.

Look for humorous ways to keep the romance alive. Try hiding little love notes where your partner doesn't expect to find them — in folded underwear or in a food item.

Create a silly song or ridiculous poem for your loved one. This is always well received because it's obvious you took the time to develop it.

Families

Humor is often the best way to express emotions. John Devaney told a story in *Modern Maturity* about Art Carney who played Ed Norton in *The Honeymooners*. In 1966 Art and Jean, his wife of twenty-six years, ended their marriage. Both remarried, but later divorced their second spouses. One Spring day in 1979, Carney showed up at their old home, where Jean was living. "I rapped on the door," he says, shifting to the side-of-the-mouth, loud voice he used as Ed Norton. "I said, 'I'm home. What's for dinner?' She said, 'Come on in.'" The Carneys remarried.

If you are in a family situation, one of the greatest gifts you can impart to your children is the gift of this sixth sense. Like most parents, if I had to do it

164

over again, there are some things in the area of child-rearing I would do differently. But the one area in which I have no regrets, the one of which I am most proud and derive the greatest satisfaction, is indoctrinating them with a sense of humor. All three of my daughters have tremendous sixth senses and I am reminded weekly just how well this serves them in so many ways. They are popular, they deal well with stressful situations and they have good perspectives on adversity.

"If I were given the opportunity to present a gift to the next generation, it would be the ability for each individual to laugh at himself."
— Charles Schultz

It is difficult to overstate the importance of instilling a sense of humor in children. It begins early with peekaboo and progresses to wordplay. From the earliest moments of life, a baby's smile and then its laugh are forms of communication. All these signs of joy require the appropriate response from parents and care-givers. Our response to this behavior determines whether the child goes on chuckling or stops. Encouragement will mean the child will be much more likely to be a fun-loving person. A newborn reacts to talking, singing, rocking and funny faces as well as sounds such as chimes, rattles and music; and physical play such as tickling and cuddling. What they laugh at is a reliable means of gauging his or her development. It provides an insight into their understanding of the world.

They find things funny that are beyond our appreciation. The word "poop," for instance, seems to be amusing to children. Poop jokes are funny to them for the same reason that dirty jokes are funny to adults. It is their way of dealing with taboo subjects. Humor is often iconoclastic and this is a child's method of finding humor in the forbidden.

"Every human being either adds to or subtracts from the happiness of those with whom he or she comes into contact."
—Anon.

Watching a child develop his sense of humor is a way of observing the acquisition of cognitive skills. They invariably move from crib humor to humor based on incongruity — demonstrating their capability of abstract thinking. From here they will progress to humor based on linguistic and logic skills — such as riddles and other wordplay. The parents' participation and enthusiastic feedback will foster attributes that will contribute to family cohesiveness and carry them into success as adults. They will learn to laugh at life's incongruities, deal with stress and frustration, solve problems and relate to their peers successfully. Humor is also a good way to send messages to a child. This works much better than nagging.

Harpo Marx's son Bill, relates how his dad engendered a sense of humor in his family. At dinnertime, he would begin his nightly ritual by raising his forefinger and saying, "And in conclusion . . ." This was the signal for everyone to go around the table and review their highs and lows of the day. Harpo would take the gripes and reduce them to absurdity. Soon everyone was laughing at themselves and the problems faded away. This exemplifies the adage that the higher your stress level — at work or at home — the more humor you need.

Candice Bergen's father, ventriloquist and comedian Edgar Bergen, instilled in her an appreciation for humor. She relates how he would sit with her for hours, going over cartoons and asking her to explain what was funny. She likened it to a humor seminar and says she has tried to impart the same love of humor to her daughter.

Yakov Smirnoff is a Russian émigré who makes jokes about what a wonderful country America is. He says he realized he was funny at age six. He relates how his family shared a small apartment in Moscow with seventeen people. Since there was no privacy, when his parents wanted to make love, his father would tell him to look out the window. Once his dad asked him what he saw. He said he was watching the neighbors making love. His dad asked him how he knew that and he told him, "Because their son is looking out their bedroom window." When he heard his parents telling his relatives and laughing, he realized how funny it was.

Close families laugh, joke and play harmless and humorous tricks on each other. Take a banana from your family fruit bowl and carefully cut into the skin, removing the fruit. Then place a wiener in its place and use translucent glue to reseal it. Place it back in the fruit bowl. If you don't think your family will appreciate it, take your reconstituted banana back to the supermarket.

Uniting the family with humor

Because I grew up with lots of humor, it's difficult for me to imagine a home without laughter. Humor is the best antidote to life's trials and tribulations. Laughter in the home is its heartbeat. It fuels the warmth we share. It brings light to the dark corridors of our life. When I was growing up in Canton, Ohio, there was a store that specialized in joke gadgets. I would buy fake vomit and pretend to throw up at home. Or I'd purchase a false thumb that looked smashed and then put it on and go into the house pretending to have banged it. This nearly drove my mother nuts but my parents would play good-natured jokes on me as well. No wonder I have a good sense of humor! Last Mother's Day I sent in to Stonyfield Farm and had my mom sent her own Adopt-A-Cow Kit, which included a signed certificate inscribed with her name and the cow's name, the cow's personal biography, a photo of Bossie, and a twice-yearly *moos*-letter. The advertisement for this kit claimed there was no better *whey* to celebrate the occasion.

Actress Jamie Lee Curtis has established a birthday tradition for her mother, actress Janet Leigh. According to an article in *Readers Digest*, every year on Curtis's birthday at 8:36 a.m., she calls her mom and mimics a birthing coach. "All right, Janet. Come on. Keep pushing. Breathe in. There you go!" Then, at 8:37 she begins to wail like a newborn. She thanks her mother for pushing so hard. What a neat idea: calling your mother to thank her for your existence.

My youngest daughter tended to have a sloppy bedroom and to dress the same way. I once posted a sign on her bedroom that read, "Stay Out — bomb testing site." I sent away for a T-shirt that read: "Bag Lady Academy." She still has the shirt. Although torn and tattered, she treasures it today.

"Laughter has no age. It belongs to all generations — especially when it is shared. That's the secret of crossing the generation gap."
—Bob Talbert

Here are a few more traditional things you can do to instill a sense of humor in your children:
1) Laugh often *with* them.
2) Remember and relate the rules that apply to the use of humor, and be aware that children sometimes have different interpretations of words and phrases. ("He got kicked out." A child will often envision someone being literally booted out the door!)
3) Encourage constructive humorous expression.
4) Keep in mind that humorous preferences will change as your child matures.
5) Teach your child to play with words. (Word games help build expansive vocabularies — even if the words are nonsensical.)
6) Read the funny papers to them.
7) React positively to their humor. (Remember usage rather than quality is important.)
8) Make up funny stories to tell them (such as at bedtime).
9) Explain to them what is *not* funny (such as ridiculing or demeaning humor).
10) Remember that the bottom line is *exposure* and *encouragement.*
11) Help them to see the humor in their own actions and foibles.

"You grow up the first day you have your first real laugh — at yourself"
—Ethel Barrymore

Having a humorous outlook on life will allow children to deal with rejection. Remember that humor is the ability to think funny and laugh at yourself. An example of these two traits and how they apply in this context is captured in the true anecdote about Groucho Marx. He once became interested in a swim club and inquired about a membership. When he learned that he would not be able to join because he was Jewish, Groucho, whose wife was a Gentile, asked if they would let his son go into the water up to his knees.

"If you carry your childhood with you, you never become older"
—Abraham Sutzkever

Friendships

Here are some ideas you can use to have fun with your friends: Get one of those picture frames you see in museums or homes holding fine paintings — the one with a light that shines on the picture. Hang it in a conspicuous place in your house. When you are expecting a friend to visit, place their picture in it. They will see their photo being held in such esteem, it is sure to get a laugh.

At Christmastime, I used to get lots of sample greeting cards from companies wanting to customize them for me. The samples came with standard messages but with a notation where you would normally sign your name. It read: "Your company's name here." I used to sent them out with that notation crudely scratched out and my name above it. This past Christmas I came up with another way to spread some joy in the form of good natured humor. I normally get at least a couple of those family newsletters — usually from rather distant business colleagues and other folks I hardly know. This year I took one and the family photograph that always accompanies it and sent it on to my friend in Las Vegas. It was attached to a brief letter pretending to be from the family whose photo was included.

The note said,

> *"Dear Cork, Carolyn and Puck: (Puck is their dog)*
> *We are doing fine, as you can see from the attached letter. The family remains in good health. We do miss you and we must get together soon. Why don't the three of you come down and stay with us. Or, since we've been wanting to come to Las Vegas anyway, we'll come over and stay with you. The only thing is, besides being very cluttered,*

your house is too small. A better idea would be for us to
round up the gang and come up in our trailer which we
could park in your yard.

Do you have a toilet hookup there? If not, maybe you
could put one in during the holidays — or just dig a hole
in your front yard. Take care of that. We'll be stopping in
after the first of the year.

Humor columnist Dave Barry says he removed a sign from a Hyatt Hotel that tells guests they will be charged $75 for stealing their towels and put it in his own bathroom to amuse his friends.

My own house has a sign above the dining counter that reads:

Historical Marker
On February 26, 1994 the Dirty dishes in
the sink below reached this elevation

In addition to making life more exciting and fun, developing and using your sense of humor will strengthen your friendships and enhance your romantic relationships.

Send your friends a letter purporting to be from a company or governmental district advising them that a new sewer line is going to be laid in front of their property to carry raw sewerage. Tell them that there will be extensive digging resulting in lots of dirt, dust and a horrible stench. Ask for their patience for a extended period. Or call up a friend and, pretending to be a telephone lineman (lineperson?), tell them you are going to blow out the line and that they should leave the phone off the hook and cover it with a towel so that dirt won't get all over the place.

Here's a letter I often send to friends:

House of Prayer Rescue Mission
1550 Market Ave.
San Diego, CA 92101

Dear Bill:

Perhaps you've heard of me and my nationwide
crusade. I preach throughout the country on the evils of
boozing, carousing and excessive sexual promiscuousness.

Accompanying me on these tours is my longtime
companion, Clyde. Clyde is a pathetic case. As I discuss
this kind of depraved and immoral behavior, Clyde sits at

my side on the platform, wheezing, coughing, flatuating, slobbering and fondling himself. He is a perfect example of a lifetime of smoking, boozing, chasing women and excessive sexual self-abuse and serves to demonstrate the results of this kind of lifestyle.

Unfortunately, last week Clyde died, and I was wondering if you would consider taking his place on my forthcoming tour.

Please let me know if you can join me and help in our struggle against licentiousness, alcoholism and debauchery.

Sincerely,
Rev. Billy Joe McMannus

One friend, in responding to the letter (they all seemed to know it was sent by me!) sent the following note: "It was so good hearing from you. I do value our friendship, particularly since you are one of the few people in this world that I feel superior to."

I enjoy playing humorous pranks on my friends and they seem to enjoy it too. I had a close friend (he recently died) who was Slovakian. A few years ago I took the plastic top from a six-pack of beer and stapled it to a small thin board. I sent it to him with a letter explaining that I was one of a large team of Slovakian scientists who wanted him to try out their newly-developed fly swatter. A mutual friend called me to say that he took it everywhere showing it to people. I don't have to tell you he had a great sense of humor.

Friendly pranks

When I lived in Modesto, California, our family had a friend who was a bachelor and who particularly enjoyed eating pistachio nuts and drinking Coors beer. Every year on Easter my wife and I would make an Easter basket full of his favorite beer and a large bag of his favorite nuts along with a note from the Easter Bunny. We put it on his doorstep in the middle of the night so he would find it on Easter morning. He never knew who his benefactor was until, just before we left town, we told him. Since he had few friends, his Easter basket was always special to him.

As a professional put-on artist, I appear before audiences around the country in fictitious roles. In selecting my identity, I often use names of old friends I haven't seen in a while and who don't know about my spoofs. I do a fake biography for the client, which they use to place in their programs to set up the ruse. I then send my old friend a copy of the biography with an anonymous note telling them I'll be there or questioning their education or some such thing. I get a chuckle out of imagining their reaction.

Good friends do these kinds of things. They play tricks on their pals. I recall how my best friend once relayed his best wishes for my birthday. My wife and I received a bouquet of flowers. She quite naturally thought they were for her. But when she opened the card, she found a message to me from my buddy: "Happy birthday, you big sweetheart!"

Do you have friends or relatives who have approached you with the Amway or another multilevel marketing (MLM) scheme? Here's a good way to have some fun with them or any of your friends and relatives. Pretending to be serious, sit them down and try to recruit them (with a straight face) into a MLM cryogenics plan. I went down to the local convenience store where they have a machine that will produce a dozen business cards for a couple of dollars. I had them printed with my name and a fictitious company called Nu-Life Cryogenics. Then I would try to get friends to join this scheme involving freezing your body prior to death and storing it for later retrieval and reconstruction. (There are people doing this, albeit not on a MLM arrangement — that I know of!)

I saw an advertisement in the newspaper that someone took out for their friend. It said,

Nelson Holland:

A Half Century of Accomplishment

- *Only baby ever born in Gary, Indiana with a crew cut — and he's still sporting it.*

- *Received scholarship to Miami of Florida. Enrolled at Miami of Ohio by mistake.*

- *Only man in history to try out with the poor old St. Louis Browns and not make the team.*

- *Joined Samuel Burrows Co. in Cleveland, causing stock to fall 53 points.*

- *Set record for most tennis racquets smashed in a single year — 7.*

- *Holds record for most consecutive days in a button-down shirt.*

- *Scored hole-in-one at Camelback Golf Course, but finished with the highest score in the tournament.*

- *Wrote bestselling sham, "How to Make a Killing in Avocados."*
- *Sea World's Shamu invited him to dinner. Bob was the main course.*

This ad (I changed some of names) can be replicated and used for one of your friends. Just follow the format, using items that apply to his/her background.

On one of my *significant* birthdays, I made a journey back to my hometown of Canton to revisit some of the sites where I spent my childhood. My brother and sister both met me at the airport. When I came into the terminal they were waiting for me — with a wheelchair!

I often visit garage sales and purchase humorous gifts for such occasions. Things like walkers. They are excellent gifts for friends celebrating advanced birthdays. Other gifts implying infirmity are also good to give people at birthday commemorations. The point is to use the same ideas mentioned in other chapters here to be attentive but different. Instead of sending the usual get-well card, design a gift certificate from Dr. Jack Kervorkian and mail it to a friend.

Of course, in romance we like to have a lover who is also a friend and good companion. People often wonder about the difference between a friend and good companion. A friend is someone who is loyal, trustworthy and reliable. These are the qualities you look for in a confidante. A good companion is one who is fun to be with. They normally share our interests (at least in whatever it is we're doing at the time we're with them). But one is not necessarily the other. Good companionship is when one's inner-child relates well with the other's inner-child.

> *"Tell me what you laugh at and I'll tell you what you are."*
> —Bob Ross

And before we leave friendships, let us not forget the most important one — that which most influences the quality of your life. It's important to be a good friend to yourself. If you are happy with yourself, you will carry a more positive attitude and this will be reflected in all aspects of your life. A humorous outlook on life will help give you a healthy perspective and provide self-energizing behavior.

Chapter Ten

Master The Art of Living & Laughing

"Humor is a metaphoric umbrella for all of the positive emotions:
joy, hope, will to live, determination, festivity"
—Norman Cousins

The following is a poem from a memorial service announcement:

I'd like the memory of me to be a happy one.
I'd like to leave an afterglow of smiles when life is done.
I'd like to leave an echo whispering softly down the ways,
Of happy times and laughing times and bright and sunny days.
I'd like the tears of those who grieve, to dry before the sun.
Of happy memories that I leave, when life is done.

— Marie Pfeifer

There is an old saying that life is too important to be taken seriously. We ought to go out as we lived. When famous humorist Dorothy Parker died, her epitaph was most appropriate — "Excuse my dust." Comedian W.C. Fields asked that his tombstone read, "All things considered, I'd rather be in

Philadelphia." John Barrymore left his legacy in an epitaph stating, "Pardon me for not standing." Capsulizing one's life on a tombstone ranges from the bizarre to the sublime. Here are a couple of other humorous epitaphs — a Wisconsin lawyer: "The defense rests." An anonymous baker: "All the yeast in the world couldn't make him rise again."

Obviously, not all epitaphs are created by the deceased. Many are written by the loved ones left behind. When lengendary pool hustler Minnesota Fats (real name, Rudolf Wanderone) died, his widow, Theresa, created his epitaph: "Beat everybody living on Earth. Now, St. Peter, rack 'em up." Oliver Hardy's epitaph reads, "A genius of comedy. His talent brought joy and laughter to the world." And the unforgettable Marty Feldman leaves us this legacy — "He made us laugh, he took my pain away."

And here's a very candid obituary from the *New York Times*: "Those who remember our cofounder mourn his passing and are certain he considers this a sentimental waste of money."

Some other humorously clever and anonymous epitaphs we've seen:
"A Day Late and a Dollar Shor,"
"I'd rather be hunting and fishing"
"I'm having the time of my life!"

Checking out with a chuckle

"Dying is easy; comedy is difficult."

—Edmund Kean

When Trampie the Clown died, his pallbearers came to his funeral in St. Paul, Minnesota, wearing red and yellow wigs, wide orange ties, outlandish pants and huge shoes.

The folks from the funeral industry seem to realize that these changing times call for some latitude in attitude. One cemetery agreed to let a car lover share his eternal parking spot with his beloved 1984 white Corvette. The cremated remains of George Swanson were buried in the driver's seat of his Corvette, which bears the license plate "HI-PAL." Swanson bought twelve burial plots at the cemetery to make sure he'd fit.

Some cemeteries use humor in their promotions. One in Chicago sponsors 10k "Heaven Can Wait" runs and offers discounts based on points scored by the Chicago Bulls basketball team.

"The most wasted day of all is that in which we have not laughed."

—Sebastien Roch Nicolas Chamfort

A company in Des Moines, Iowa, will sprinkle your departed loved one's ashes over his favorite golf course. One hacker's will requested that he be buried under a tee marker with the inscription, "He's *finally* keeping his head down." While some folks opt for a tasteful urn, others wish their earthly remains to be scattered over a beloved swatch of land or stretch of ocean. A fellow in North Carolina directed that his funeral be conducted at a spot where he spent his Saturdays shooting targets. Following his instructions, friends and relatives each blasted a shotgun with twelve to twenty gauge shells filled with his ashes.

There are specialty funeral directors who are into the lighter side of dying. A Palatine, Illinois, mortuary has a miniature golf course in his basement. Between funerals, players try to negotiate a nine-hole layout featuring such obstacles as a metal skull with blinking red eyes, a guillotine, a faux pinball machine with tombstone bumpers and a water hazard inhabited by rubber alligators.

The York Group, Inc. is the nation's second largest hardwood and metal casket manufacturer. They have plants all around the country and produce 450,000 caskets a year. Now they've reportedly introduced a new model that comes with a felt tip pen. It's a graffiti coffin made of white ash and designed for mourners to scribble farewell notes to the deceased on it. George Foley Jr., their executive vice president, says that it is in response to a growing demand within the funeral business for services that permit the mourner to feel more a part of the farewell. The company also markets Velcro-cloth casket inserts depicting everything from pastoral tractor-and-silo farm tableaus, including flags and fish, to a scene of one of the golf holes at Augusta National.

In an article about the more bizarre aspects of the funeral business, one mortician recalled the special biker funeral service where friends and relatives of the deceased paid tribute by relieving themselves into his grave site.

Las Vegas is the home of Palm Mortuaries where they will go to any lengths to comply with requests, however strange. One example — they allowed survivors to paint a coffin with bright orange racing stripes. Their roadside billboard is in keeping with their less than traditional approach to death. It reads, "Don't drink and drive. We'd rather wait."

Safe at home

In other cases, relatives are more than accommodating. Eddie Ellner, a writer from Santa Monica, carried out the dying wish of his grandmother. Before she died in 1990, Betty Fein made her grandson promise that if the Yankees won the World Series again, he would scatter her ashes across the field at Yankee Stadium. So after the team beat the Atlanta Braves, Ellner boarded a plane for New York with a rose-colored marble urn containing Fein's ashes. Since he knew he'd never be able to get through security on his own, he hooked up with a photographer and scattered her ashes on home plate, the on-deck circle, along the first base line and in the infield grass at the stadium. Mark Gruenwald of Marvel Comics requested that his ashes be blended with ink and used in a 1985 series of collector's editions. Bob Harras, the magazine's editor-in-chief reacted with the comment, "He wanted to be a part of his work in a very real sense."

For myself, I'd like to play off the often-heard statement that you've never seen a hearse pulling a U-Haul. At the tail-end of my funeral procession (or, right behind the hearse) I'd like to have a Brinks' truck. No sign or other message would be necessary. People would see it and the ah ha factor would kick in. What a way to go! Then, as my epitaph, I'd like either, "Is it hot in here, or is it me?" or "Take the flowers and bring me some bug spray."

You needn't be as flamboyant as all these folks or me, but if you've lived life displaying a good sense of humor, you might want to go out in a similar style. If your life and your relationships have been full of fun and laughter, why go to your final destination without leaving a legacy of laughter? Leave a farewell reflective of the life you've led. Besides, a little humor will help your loved ones begin the healing process. So don't drown them in sorrow; let them soar in the vibrancy of your life. They'll think "I miss him/her because (s)he always made me laugh!" It will make them think of the times you sang, danced and laughed together. Leave some legacy of laughter so that after the flowers have wilted, you can make some appearances "post-humorously!"

Here's a ditty I once saw. It was attributed to United Technologies Corp.:

"Most of us miss out on life's big prizes such as the Pulitzer, the Nobel. Oscars, Tonys and Emmys. But we're all eligible for life's small pleasures. A pat on the back. A kiss behind the ear. A four-pound bass. A full moon. An empty parking space. A crackling fire. A great meal. A glorious sunset. Hot soup. Cold beer. Don't fret about copping life's grand awards. Enjoy its tiny delights. There are plenty for all of us."

"A man isn't really poor if he can still laugh."

—Anon.

Myths

And don't believe all the myths just because life is full of them. Ostriches don't really bury their heads in the sand; Marie Antoinette never said, "Let them eat cake," Bogart never said, "Play it again, Sam" and a lion tamer doesn't actually *tame* lions, he simply manipulates space. But, by far, the biggest myth is that wealth creates happiness.

In 1988 Buddy Post of Pittsburgh won $16.2 million in the Pennsylvania Lottery. Since then, his life has become a nightmare. Among other things, his wife has left him, his brother has been convicted of trying to kill him and his landlady has successfully sued him for one-third of the jackpot. The mansion he bought with his winnings is half-filled with paperwork from bankruptcy proceedings and lawsuits and the gas has been shut off. Another fellow won $18.6 million in the lottery. He recently died after a 20-month binge on cigarettes,

drink and fast food, according to the tabloid *Sun* newspaper. Ernie Bailey, a 63-year-old former factory worker, apparently ignored his doctor's advice to stop indulging and had ballooned to 310 pounds by the time he died in the luxury bungalow he bought after his April, 1995, bonanza.

Money created more problems than it solved for Ernie and Buddy and that would be the case for most people in the same situation.

Many people spend their entire life chasing money and material wealth in the mistaken belief that more will mean happiness. The problem is that they are playing a game they can't win. It seems you can never have enough money. The more you get, the more you want, so you are always reaching.

Being rich really isn't even about having money. An item in *Reader's Digest* offered this advice about "being rich." It first discussed the amount of money needed in contemporary society to be considered rich. Then Benjamin J. Stein wrote: "But I keep thinking of how many people I know with far more than that who do not seem happy. On the other hand, I know many people who have trouble paying their bills yet are really well-off.

"If you can share any problem with your wife, you're rich. If you can face your parents and believe you have given back to them even a hint of what they gave you, you're rich. If you can take an afternoon off to go boating with your pal, you're rich. If you can honestly say you have nothing to hide, you are really, really rich."

"Happiness is different from pleasure. Happiness has something to do with struggling and enduring and accomplishing."

—George Sheehan

The bottom line

Real wealth is about being happy! Unless you are into some form of intentional suffering or planned self-denial, what we all seek in life is happiness. Happiness has been the subject of philosophers over the centuries. Lately, it has come under a great deal of scientific study. The prevailing theory emerging from these scientific approaches is that we are predisposed toward a certain level of happiness and we can't do a lot about it. A recent paper published in the journal *Psychological Science* states that "trying to be happier is as futile as trying to be taller, and therefore is counterproductive." This theory holds that we all have a genetic set point which controls our level of happiness over the long run. We may rise above or fall below this preset value, researchers found, but we will invariably return to the mood level it represents in the same way we have a metabolic set point that governs our weight. This biologically-based temperament is thought to be passed down as a complex pattern of interacting genes that control the brain chemicals serotonin and dopamine, both associated with pleasure and mood.

Lance Armstrong was a 25-year-old world-class bicycle racer when doctors diagnosed testicular cancer that had spread to his lungs and appeared to be fatal. Through chemotherapy and other treatment he survived and the cancer went into remission. Lance says he only has two kinds of days; good and great. He says cancer was probably the greatest thing that ever happened to him. It gave him a new and valuable perspective on life.

Scientists studying happiness in several countries have found that money seems to have little to do with a person's level of happiness (except among the very poor). Education doesn't count for much either; nor do marriage, a family

178

or any of the other variables that researchers have sought to correlate with contentment. Each factor may make a person a little happier, they submit, but it will have a minor impact, compared with the individual's characteristic sense of well-being. They have data that shows lottery winners are no happier a year after their good fortune than they were before. And several studies show that even people with spinal-cord injuries tend to rebound in spirits. Happiness is clearly and solely a perception.

David T. Lykken, a behavioral scientist at the University of Minnesota, studied 1,500 pairs of twins. He compared how pairs of fraternal and identical twins rate their sense of well-being. This set-point concept indicates that about half of a person's sense of well-being is decided by a genetically determined set-point and the other half is from the sorrows and pleasures of the last few hours, days or weeks. Lykken and his colleagues believe that the distribution of happiness is stochastic (random). As a result of that study and others like it, some scientists believe we can develop precision mood drugs — designer versions of Prozac. Then, according to Dean Hamer of the National Institute of Health, "Everybody will be happier!"

"Laughter is just inner happiness coming to the top of the bottle."
—Anon.

But skeptics argue that while these studies measure some element of temperament, they do not address the more elusive quality of happiness which may never be reduced to the workings of genetics and chemistry.

Well, so much for Aristotle who believed that happiness could be found in a life of intellectual contemplation. And so much for all the generations of theologians who equated happiness with nearness to God. And that's it for Hippocrates who, in the fifth century B.C., believed happiness would be achieved when the "four humours" are in balance. Another ancient Greek philosopher proposed that the surest route to happiness was not by obtaining those things we want but by not wanting those things we don't have. And so much for those prevailing hordes who believe that happiness is a function of economics.

Getting a handle on happiness

I am convinced that happiness can be enhanced substantially by the individual. It may, and probably does, take a sustained effort to achieve a lasting result, but you *can* elevate your own sense of happiness. I am an advocate of Freud's philosophy that happiness is a result of love and work.

It is helpful to understand the basics of happiness — what it is and what it is not. Most people labor under the belief that it is the end result of a good job or a lucrative financial station in life.

Happiness is a choice. We almost always make it a subconscious choice rather than a conscious one. But it is a *choice we make*. We actually choose whether we will be happy. Just knowing that we decide for ourselves how happy we are going to be is a good beginning in elevating our level of happiness. The choice to be happy takes the same amount of time that one uses to choose to be unhappy.

Happiness is not getting what we want, it is wanting what we get. Nearly all the people I've talked to believe that winning the lottery would bring great happiness into their lives. Few appreciate that it would actually create more problems than it would solve. (Not that problems are a hindrance to happiness; they are fodder for achieving it!) It is not, as mentioned above, a matter of material things. Wayne Dyer, author of several books on self-improvement, suggests a revealing exercise. Make a list all the material things you really value. Then, identify which of those you would be willing to die for. Now list your friends and loved-ones and the values you really cherish. This will give you a renewed and healthy perspective about "values."

Happiness is strongly connected to positive moods and an optimistic state of mind. These are prerequisites to obtaining food, shelter, social support and mating opportunities as well as the general state of happiness. They are also thought to motivate human sociability, exploration and creativity, and produce a healthy immune system. So developing and maintaining these states of mind have numerous precious benefits.

Happiness is not a state to arrive at, but a manner of traveling. All happiness is fleeting. Just as sadness and depression are cured with time, so it is with happiness. Happiness, like success, is not a destination but a journey.

Happiness is an inside job. As William James, the eminent American philosopher and educator noted, "the greatest discovery of our generation is that happiness is not a matter of worldly possessions or good fortune but a state of mind—a mental attitude, and that human beings, by changing the inner attitudes of their minds, can change the outer aspects of their lives."

> *"Things turn out best for those who make the best*
> *of the way things turn out."*
>
> —Anon.

Radio talk show host Rush Limbaugh gives listeners a quiz. Two children each have six crayons. The first child has broken one-third of her crayons while the second child has broken one-half of his. Which child should be the saddest? People typically answer, "the second child." But it is a trick question. When they respond, Limbaugh lectures them that children should not be sad over crayons under any circumstances. Moreover, he explains, one can color with a broken crayon. He decries this kind of thinking — tying such trivial things to happiness. I am not a fan of Limbaugh, but when he's right he's right.

Children often get a twisted perspective. When one of the members of the "Spice Girls" left that musical group, a New York newspaper rustled up a group of psychologists and ran an article dispensing advice on how parents should deal with their children's trauma created by the departure.

The happiest people

The Gallup Organization took a poll of eighteen nations to discover who were the happiest people. It turned out to be Icelanders. While there are fewer than 300,000 of them, 82 percent are satisfied with their personal lives. This compares to 72 percent in the U.S., which ranked fifth, and only 42 percent of the Japanese, who came in seventh. Researchers examined various aspects of life in Iceland in an attempt to find out why they are so blissful. The bottom line is they have limited expectations and they tend to enjoy what they do have.

Enjoying what we have means focusing on today, rather than reliving yesterday or planning tomorrow. Most of us could enjoy life more if we savored the moment.

"Nothing is worth more than this day."

—Goethe

As Groucho Marx used to say to himself when he opened his eyes each morning: "I, not events, have the power to make me happy or unhappy today. I can choose which it shall be. Yesterday is dead, tomorrow hasn't arrived yet. I have just one day, today, and I'm going to be happy in it."

Yesterday is a canceled check.

Tomorrow is a promissory note.

Today is all the cash you have!

After all, life is about depth, not length. Most thinking people would rather live a rich and fulfilling life for a shorter period of time rather than a longer but uneventful, boring and unfulfilling one.

Actor Michael Landon, who died prematurely of pancreatic cancer, knew he didn't have long to live. In contemplating his death he said, "It isn't like I didn't live a rich and fulfilling life!" He obviously recognized the notion of life being more about depth than length. Where do you get depth? It is comprised (at least for me) of friendships, romance, fun, fellowship and fulfillment. Shallow lives are usually devoid of these things.

> *"God's greatest gift to man is the joy of laughter.*
> *We laugh before we speak — we laugh before we walk."*
>
> —Ken Murray

Reader's Digest contained an item submitted by Tony Campolo who offered this bit of wisdom on the matter: "Most of us are tiptoeing through life so we can reach death safely. Don't be satisfied with just pumping blood."

Consider this from Friedrich Nietzsche: "What if a demon were to creep after you one night, in your loneliest loneness, and say, 'This life which you live must be lived by you once again and innumerable times more; and every pain and joy and thought and sigh must come again to you, all in the same sequence. The eternal hourglass will again and again be turned — and you with it, dust of the dust!' Would you throw yourself down and gnash your teeth and curse that demon? Or would you answer, 'Never have I heard anything more divine'?"

Have a Life Plan

> *"Life is a journey. Enjoy the ride!"*
>
> —Nissan commercial

You wouldn't think of going into business or embarking on a journey or other venture without a plan. So it is helpful to your state of happiness that you have some kind of blueprint to ensure a maximum level of happiness in your life.

Several years ago I saw a list of New Year's Resolutions which I thought were excellent and useful year-around. I believe they are a rather succinct formula for success at the art of living and I try to review them each year and make them a part of *my life plan*:

1) Take care of yourself. Good health is everyone's major source of wealth. Without it, happiness is almost impossible.
2) Resolve to be cheerful and helpful. People will repay you in kind.
3) Avoid angry, abrasive persons. They are generally vengeful.
4) Avoid zealots. They are generally humorless.
5) Resolve to listen more and talk less. No one ever learns anything by talking.
6) Be chary of giving advice. Wise men don't need it, and fools won't heed it.

7) Resolve to be tender with the young, compassionate with the aged, sympathetic with the striving and tolerant of the weak and the wrong. Sometime in your life you will have been all of these.

8) Do not equate money with success. There are many successful money-makers who are miserable failures as human beings. What counts most about success is how a person achieves it.

In regard to point number one, it is important to look at people and things "on balance." Good health, for example, does not mean perfect health. So it should be evaluated on balance. It is certainly possible to be happy and in poor health, but it is most difficult. W. Mitchell is a professional speaker I've had the pleasure of meeting. Mr. Mitchell had the misfortune of being in a severe motorcycle accident which burned a large part of his body. He then survived a terrible airplane crash. The result of these two accidents is a wheelchair-bound disfigured man who exudes happiness. But he is extremely rare. His philosophy is, "I don't count the thousands of things I *can't* do; I count the millions of things I *can* do." Mr. Mitchell is a delightful fellow, worthy of studying and emulating, whether you're in good health or in poor health.

"Time spent laughing is time spent with the gods."
—Japanese proverb

It's kind of sad to know that there are twenty-four hours in a day and only one is referred to as the "Happy Hour."

Here are a few ways that I try to ensure that I'm maximizing my happiness potential. First, when I get up in the morning, I stretch and then say, "I'm healthy, I'm happy, I'm here for fun." On my mirror in the bedroom I have an item that I cut out of a magazine. It is a column containing the obituaries of several men. When I first read the article I realized they all had something in common. They were all wealthy, well-known and powerful men. And they were all dead. It occurred to me that each one of those fellows would give up all their wealth, all their power and everything else they had to live *just through today*. I have that day! It's that precious. I try to keep that thought throughout the day.

When I sit down with my morning coffee and open the newspaper I turn first to the obituaries. I quickly scan them noting ages, cause of death and so on. This reinforces the earlier thought and also gives me a good perspective as I read the news and determine to make the most of my day.

"Humor is the great thing, the saving thing. The minute it crops up, all our irritations and resentments slip away, and a sunny spirit takes their place."
—Mark Twain

A pilot friend of mine told me that he can get up in the morning and find a bleary, dreary overcast day. But when he jumps in his airplane and flies above the clouds, the sun is shining and it's a lovely day. Humor takes us on a similar trip above the clouds to live in the sunshine! I try to find some humor to begin my day — to take me up *above the clouds* and, as the poem says, "to touch the hand of God." It epitomizes Dorothy's line in the last scene of *The Wizard of Oz* when she says, we'd find happiness right in our own back yard.

I'm not a particularly religious person but I do have a prayer I try to repeat daily:

"I acknowledge just how fortunate I am to be alive and well and to enjoy another day on this planet. It doesn't matter that— (and here I fill in my current concern — whatever it is that might be troubling me at the moment).

"Whether and just how much I enjoy this day will be up to me. Happiness is a choice. It is an inside job! No one else can create my happiness.

"My fortune is not now and never will be in money or material wealth. I am in good health and unlike most of the people in this world, I have all the necessities of life. And, like only a very few, I have the good fortune to be living my vocational dream.

"Knowing that what goes around, comes around, I will try to spread happiness today. I will smile frequently and try to laugh often.

"I will be aware of my tendencies toward unrealistic expectations and my limited patience. I will be tolerant of the ignorant and the weak, as I have frequently been both during my lifetime.

"My day will be filled with the thought that I am healthy, I'm happy and I'm here for fun!"

I try to repeat my mantra several times during the day. "I'm healthy, I'm happy, I'm here for fun." Then I try to take the good things that happen to me during the day, whether they be a good meal, a sip of fine wine or laughing with a friend, and savor it. The next time you're enjoying an apple or some ice cream, instead of just eating it as usual, try savoring it and see if it doesn't taste better and you don't derive more joy from it than you would otherwise.

When adversity comes my way and I experience a setback, I try to say, "So what?" I try to resist the temptation to overreact and remind myself that it's not very important as things go. Making the most of what comes and the least of what goes is another way of expressing what songwriter Johnny Mercer championed in his verse "accentuate the positive, eliminate the negative." Savoring the finer moments of life and putting the less desirable ones into perspective cannot, in my opinion, help but enhance your happiness quotient. Several of my friends who developed cancer or another of those dreaded deadly diseases confided to me, "Gee, to think of the things I worried about before this happened to me!" All their worries paled beside life's *real* tragedy.

> *"All the animals, excepting man, know that the*
> *principal business of life is to enjoy it."*
> —Samuel Butler

We seem to attend to the mundane activities of life such as going to work, eating and sleeping; but most of us spend very little time tuning up our sense of humor and reinforcing our attitudes so that we are getting the most from life. Between the flushing and the flossing, take time to rededicate yourself to enjoying life and the people around you.

Back to the future

> *"The proper function of man is to live, not to exist."*
> —Jack London

I recently read some philosophy provided by an 85-year-old woman. She was lamenting how she would live her life if she had it to do again. It was along the lines of "I'd make more mistakes, climb more mountains, cross more rivers, eat more ice cream, have more actual troubles and less imaginary ones." It inspired me to make my own list, *now*, while I can still implement much of it, and then to do just that. You might want to do the same thing. Imagine you are at the edge of your existence and reflecting on how you would do it again. Make your list and then live it! That way you'll have fewer regrets later.

You've heard the adage, "You can't take it with you." Well, now a Luxembourg-based company is offering "reincarnation accounts" for the rich who would rather not start from scratch the next time around. The deal is you put up the cash (minimum $30,000) and redeem it within twenty-three years of your death by providing some key personal facts.

For myself, I'm concentrating on *this* life. People facing death don't usually fondle their bank books, think about the degrees they've earned, walk around their estate admiring it or kick the tires on their cherished car. In the end, what really matters is the circle of love. What really matters is who you loved and who loved you.

These are my ways of working at the art of living and maximizing that bottom line in my life. Perhaps some of these ideas will help you do the same. Remember, humor is an attitude—a way of responding to life!

185

Leaving a legacy of laughter

Buddy Rich, the famous drummer, was taken to the hospital in the throes of death. When the doctor asked him, "Are you allergic to anything?" he said, "Yes, country-western." Several days before his death, William Saroyan reportedly called the Associated Press with a message — "Everybody's has got to die, but I have always believed an exception would be made in my case. Now what?" Even in the face of death they didn't lose their sense of humor. Crisis is the real crucible of a sense of humor. In times of crisis, when you need it the most, it comes through for you. But it has to be there; you can't go get it when you need it.

"Dear God, take Henny, please."

—Rabbi Noach Valley
(speaking at funeral of Henny Youngman — king of the one-liners)

As George Bernard Shaw said, "Life does not cease to be funny when people die, just as it does not cease to be serious when people laugh." We certainly would be remiss if we told people to live each day to the fullest yet did not create an environment where humor is welcome.

At his funeral, Frank Sinatra's family gave him some "going away gifts." His daughter Nancy tucked a bottle of Jack Daniels whiskey in his pocket. His other daughter, Tina, slipped in a pack of Camel cigarettes and a Zippo lighter.

At the wake of San Diegan Art Damschen, his sense of humor was recalled. It seems he always carried a pocket full of engagement rings, which he handed out to any lady who caught his fancy. He then warned them not to wear the ring in the shower. When folks at the wake were asked how many of them had ever been engaged to Damschen, forty women held up their ringed hands.

The memorial service for Pete Rozelle, former commissioner of the National Football League, was sprinkled with remembrances of his "good sense of humor." His stepson Phillip Cook recalled an incident providing an example of Rozelle's humorous touch. Once, following a family birthday celebration, a restaurant employee approached Rozelle seeking his autograph on a baseball. He had obviously confused the football commissioner with baseball player Pete Rose. Rozelle responded with humor and inscribed on the baseball, "What is this thing?"

186

"You don't get to choose how you're going to die, or when. You can only decide how you're going to live. Now.
—Joan Baez

Another example of going out in the same fashion you've lived is the case of Herb Caen, the venerable San Francisco columnist. When he died in February of 1997, his eulogy was a celebration of his life. The event was replete with celebrities such as comedian Robin Williams and Mayor Willie Brown. They regaled the audience with anecdotes relating to the columnist's life. Said Williams, "This is an Episcopal church, right? Episcopal—that's Catholic Lite, same religion, half the guilt." Mayor Brown, a colorful character in his own right, got the biggest laughs with quotes from his deceased friend. One example: "Herb always said, 'It's amazing how quickly you can read my column when you're only looking for your name.'"

"I have always felt that laughter in the face of reality is probably the finest sound there is and will last until the day when the game is called on account of darkness. In this world, a good time to laugh is any time you can"
—Linda Ellerbee

When baseball Hall of Fame pitcher Don Drysdale died, more than a thousand friends, family members and fans gathered to celebrate his life in a memorial service that evoked nearly as much laughing as crying. His widow requested that family friend Bob Uecker (remember his commercial about the "cheap seats?") inject some levity into the service, "to talk about some of the lighter moments in Don's life." Said Uecker, "Don first touched me in 1961." Then, pausing for effect, pointing at his chin, "Right here. He touched me on three other occasions as well. I was brushed back by Don getting off the bus at Vero Beach once." This reminded me of another such funeral routine where the eulogizer says, "Joe touched me. He touched me for $50 not long before he died. And he put the touch on me on many other occasions too."

"We have no more right to consume happiness without producing it than to consume wealth without producing it."
—George Bernard Shaw

Dying is no time to relinquish your sense of humor. If your life has been humor rich, let your legacy reflect it. I remember reading about a doctor who had spent his life helping the poor and underprivileged and who lived above a liquor store in an impoverished area of the city. In front of the liquor store was a sign that read, "Dr. Williams Is Upstairs."

Because the doctor had never asked for any payment for treating any of his patients, he died impoverished himself. Therefore, there was no money for his burial. He had no relatives so his friends got together and scraped up enough money to have him buried. But they didn't raise enough to buy a tombstone. It appeared that his grave would remain unmarked until someone came up with a brilliant idea. They took the sign from in front of the liquor store and put it on his grave. Thus, reflecting his life, it made a wonderful epitaph — "Dr. Williams Is Upstairs."

THAT'S ALL FOLKS
The epitaph of Mel Blanc (the voice of Pork Pig)

Interested in a presentation by Bob Ross?

For more information, including
a description of Bob's presentations, contact:

Bob Ross & Associates
7559 Gibraltar Street #14
Carlsbad, CA 92009
(760) 942-1313
fax (760) 942-1555
1-888-942-1314

For additional copies of this book,
contact Bob Ross using the above information.